# ENDOF

M000280350

*The Essential Guide to the Power of the Holy Spirit* sets many God-loving people free from the bondage of the cessationism of the Holy Spirit. Dr. Randy Clark, an incredible instrument of the work of the Holy Spirit and well-versed theologian, shows breathtaking activities of the Holy Spirit in his own life, around him, and throughout the history of Christianity from its inception. Pointing to a number of miraculous healings and wonders of the very active Holy Spirit, his book will make a real impact on the reader's everyday life. This exceptionally well-balanced, inspirational, and truthful book on the power of the Holy Spirit is a must read for church leaders, including theologians.

ANDREW S. PARK
Professor of Theology and Ethics
United Theological Seminary
Dayton, OH

Dr. Randy Clark provides a valuable resource in *The Essential Guide to the Power of the Holy Spirit.* He offers practical and biblical theological wisdom from the unique position of being used by God for twenty years now all over the world in imparting outpourings of the Holy Spirit that have led to power evangelism, church planting movements, and millions of souls coming to faith in Jesus. Randy also writes with the heart of an evangelist, with pastoral wisdom, and with the careful eye of a historian of revival movements in church history. The discussion is clear and foundational, and the current day accounts of the Holy Spirit's power and gifts are exciting and inspiring. This book should be read by every person who desires to know how the Holy Spirit works in revival outpourings of power that bring souls into the Kingdom of God.

DR. GARY S. GREIG, PH.D.
Near Eastern Languages and Civilizations
The University of Chicago
Adjunct faculty, United Theological Seminary
Vice President of Biblical Content, Gospel Light Publications

Dr. Randy Clark is one of the most insightful and important Christian leaders of our day. In this readable volume, Dr. Clark offers a well-reasoned, scriptural account of the reality of the gifts of the Spirit in our own time. I highly recommend this volume for anyone who wants to learn more about the Charismatic Movement and the powerful, present work of the Holy Spirit.

DAVID F. WATSON, PH.D.
Academic Dean and Vice President for Academic Affairs
Associate Professor of New Testament
United Theological Seminary
Dayton, OH

I enjoyed reading this irenic and edifying work. Randy Clark, a veteran Charismatic leader with extensive experience in the ministry of the Spirit, rightly pleads against the misrepresentation of Charismatic Christianity. He appeals both to Scripture and subsequent history as he challenges inconsistent, postbiblical arguments, that after the Bible's completion the Spirit suddenly changed His character, or that the biblical portrayal of the Spirit's normal way of working was no longer relevant.

DR. CRAIG KEENER
Professor of New Testament
Asbury Theological Seminary

For the Charismatic who would like a guide to the Spirit and the gifts, *The Essential Guide to the Holy Spirit* by Randy Clark is extremely helpful as an apologetic with solid biblical foundations, but also practical experience from a lifelong evangelist who has ministered in the holy fire of the Spirit on every continent. This is not strange fire, as one recent book might suggest. Randy Clark carefully provides the theological arguments from various seminarians in several different Protestant and Catholic traditions. This should be required reading for some of those fundamentalist authors who believe there has been a cessation of the Holy Spirit's gifts and phenomena. I know Randy reads all his detractors, as he is so widely read, and he is gracious in the way he carefully dissects their arguments.

For instance, one recent author claims that Charismatic authors have abandoned making any attempt to correlate the modern gift of tongues with any known foreign languages. He claims *xenolalia* disappeared after Pentecost. He has not been reading Randy Clark's books, as once again Randy points out two international evangelists who were given supernatural knowledge of a foreign language. I have heard one of these men; Randy could introduce them both to a cessationist if they need more proof. And if there is a stereotype about materialistic evangelists who raise huge sums of money for personal gain, Randy could introduce the Bakers to them, as he notes in the book. And if the detractors would like to read more carefully explained theological studies comparing the longstanding position of Holy Spirit charisms versus the more recent development of fundamental dispensationalism, then Randy has a whole bookshelf of seminary texts and apologetics to offer, which he does in this book.

Randy Clark also points out that if Jonathan Edwards were still here preaching and teaching, he would look for the distinguishing marks of a true move of God. One of these is loving God through authentic worship. If any biblical figure might be guilty of wild and enthusiastic praise, it would be David as he expresses himself in numerous psalms. Even more uninhibited was his dancing and singing "*with all his might*," as the ark was returned to Israel in 2 Samuel 6. If modern detractors of wild and exuberant worship have a predecessor, it may be David's young wife Michal, who claimed, "*You have become vile in my sight.*"

I am sad and afraid for those who will not consider this type of worship holy, and this move of God as holy fire rather than strange fire. For Michal, she "*had no children unto the day of her death.*" How much fruitfulness can the next generation have if they are calling Holy Spirit worship and gifts vile in their sight? I agree with Randy that all streams in Christendom need to come together with gentler words, with unity on the basic matters of faith, so that we do not become a dry and barren land.

STEPHEN C. MORY, M.D.
Assistant Clinical Professor of Psychiatry
Vanderbilt University
Nashville, TN

# THE ESSENTIAL GUIDE TO THE POWER

## *of the*

# HOLY SPIRIT

# THE ESSENTIAL GUIDE TO THE POWER

## *of the*

# HOLY SPIRIT

### RANDY CLARK

DESTINY IMAGE® PUBLISHERS, INC.
P.O. Box 310, Shippensburg, PA 17257-0310
*"Promoting Inspired Lives."*

Cover Design by: Prodigy Pixel

This book and all other Destiny Image and Destiny Image Fiction books are available at Christian bookstores and distributors worldwide.

For more information on foreign distributors, call 717-532-3040.
Reach us on the Internet: www.destinyimage.com.

ISBN 13 TP: 978-0-7684-0605-4
ISBN 13 Ebook: 978-0-7684-0606-1

For Worldwide Distribution, Printed in the U.S.A.
2 3 4 5 6 7 8 / 19 18 17 16 15

# CONTENTS

# FOREWORD

I do not know anyone more qualified to write this book than Randy Clark. Both his grasp on church history and his understanding of Scripture helps to create the perfect platform from which to share his grasp on continuationism—the ongoing work of the Holy Spirit in the church today as in the early church. What will capture your attention most is the intimate relationship he has with the Holy Spirit. I've seen it firsthand—he lives what he teaches. God has powerfully worked through Randy's life by demonstrating miracles, signs, and wonders in the context of a life of purity and complete devotion to Christ. I've never met a more gracious and humble man whose only passion is to see God glorified in this wonderful gospel of the kingdom. This book will ignite your passion for more, and it will provide a biblical basis for what was always intended to be the normal Christian life.

BILL JOHNSON
Bethel Church, Redding, CA
Author of *When Heaven Invades Earth* and
*Hosting the Presence*

# INTRODUCTION

*The Holy Spirit is not a doctrine to be studied;*
*He is a person to be experienced in power.*

*But you will receive power when the Holy Spirit*
*comes on you; and you will be My witnesses*
*in Jerusalem, and in all Judea and Samaria,*
*and to the ends of the earth.* —Acts 1:8

*The wind blows wherever it pleases. You hear its sound,*
*but you cannot tell where it comes from or where it is going.*
*So it is with everyone born of the Spirit.* —John 3:8

## An Essential Guide to the Holy Spirit

This book is *not* the definitive guide to the Holy Spirit—His person or His power—nor is it exhaustive. I want to be careful in prefacing this book correctly, as not to give you any misinformation. However, the title was assigned intentionally. While it is not the *ultimate* guide, I believe it is an *essential* guide to the power of the Holy Spirit.

Why?

Controversy about the third person of the Trinity has been with us ever since the New Testament church was born. If anything, the more His power continues to break out in our midst, the more discussion and debate circulates around the legitimacy of these manifestations. This book has been written to give you a solid biblical framework through which to understand the power of the Spirit of God.

Initially, I constructed this work using more theological terminology. I will maintain scriptural integrity throughout the pages ahead, but I want to help break down some of these larger issues into everyday, user-friendly language.

The Holy Spirit does not exclusively belong to ivory-tower theologians; He is not a mere doctrine to be studied, but a divine

> *The Holy Spirit does not exclusively belong to ivory-tower theologians; he is not a mere doctrine to be studied, but a divine person to be experienced and known.*

person to be experienced and known. He has freely been given to *"you and your children and for all who are far off—for all whom the Lord our God will call"* (Acts 2:39). He is the wonderful gift of God poured out upon every single believer in the Lord Jesus Christ. Understanding His power and work in our lives is of vital importance if we desire to live the Christian lives that Jesus has made available to us.

The more that believers continue to stumble over the power of the Spirit through debate and controversy, the longer we as the church become restricted from bringing true transformation to our world. We cannot afford to be arguing among ourselves while there is so great and so ripe a harvest set before us in this generation.

This is why I decided to write this book on the power of the Holy Spirit. I felt that I needed to address many of the false concepts about the Holy Spirit—His movement, His activity, and, ultimately, the present-day availability of His power. Even though the latest controversies will invariably die out, it is without question that new issues will arise—same debate, different packaging. Once again, the validity of the Holy Spirit's power will be called into question and future generations will need a resource to help them correctly navigate these integral issues.

I am not at all proposing that this particular book will be the definite resource on this subject matter. However, I am offering a tool that will help you discern truth from error, and give you clarity on how the Holy Spirit desires to move in the church, in your life, and in every generation until Christ returns.

Truth be told, controversy surrounding the Holy Spirit has been around since the New Testament church emerged onto the scene in the book of Acts. In the twentieth and twenty-first centuries, it has been the works of B. B. Warfield (*Counterfeit Miracles*), Hank Hanegraaff (*Counter-*

> *We have the distinct privilege of living on earth as a people indwelt by the Holy Spirit.*

*feit Revival*), and John MacArthur *(Charismatic Chaos, Strange Fire)* that have targeted the continuing work of the Holy Spirit in respect to supernatural demonstrations of signs, wonders, miracles, healings, and other revival phenomena.

We have the distinct privilege of living on earth as a people indwelt by the Holy Spirit. As long as human flesh and the Spirit of God exist in this place of cohabitation, the unusual will continue to be commonplace. At the end of the day, we must be true to Scripture itself and address whether the Bible presents a cessationist or continuationist paradigm. Either the power of the Holy Spirit has legitimately ceased (cessationist) or Scripture affirms that it will continue to be demonstrated in our midst until the end of the age (continuationist). Neither perspective is a side issue.

Though neither cessationism nor continuationism are major theological doctrines that are mandatory for salvation, our response to either paradigm determines our level of Christian experience on this side of eternity. This is why I am confident that the journey we are going on together in the upcoming pages is not only meaningful but essential if we are to truly discover what it means to *be* a follower of the Lord Jesus Christ. Both sides of the argument—cessationist and continuationist—would acknowledge that it is the Holy Spirit alone who supernaturally enables us to follow Jesus. However, our understanding of *what* the Holy Spirit has made available to us, through His power, reveals the *extent* to which we believe we can follow Jesus in this lifetime.

> *Our understanding of what the Holy Spirit has made available to us, through His power, reveals the extent to which we believe we can follow Jesus in this lifetime.*

Here is how I have broken this work down:

I am beginning the book with a response to popular cessationist perspectives, as well as their common polemical methods. I want you to have a clear definition of what the cessationist perspective presents concerning the contemporary movement and power of the Holy Spirit.

I will continue by explaining why I believe continuationism has the proper biblical support to be accepted over cessationism. Again, I am not presenting this body of information to win a theological argument. This work is not for the purpose of debate. Rather, it is my desire to show you how vital it is to maintain a clear picture of who the Holy Spirit is and what He is able to do in your life today.

This work concludes with a valuable appendix, discussing the fruit of encounters with God, including helpful tables and figures.

In the pages ahead, I have endeavored to provide solid, biblical responses and sources for many of the subjects addressed. I hope you will use the endnotes I have included for further study related to the various subjects dealt with in this response.

## STRENGTHENED TO TAKE ACTION

*The people who know their God will display strength and take action.* (Daniel 11:32 NASB)

As you step into a greater knowledge of who the Holy Spirit is and how He continues to powerfully work in the world today, my hope is that you will become a believer who is strengthened to take action. Consider the implications of believing that God does *not* move miraculously as His normative practice in the world today. This presents a cosmic clockmaker view, which the whole of Scripture utterly rejects. Even more discouraging is that such a view pictures an impersonal deity who is disinterested in His creation, and, ultimately, disengaged from your everyday life. This is *not* your God—quite the opposite, in fact.

God personally and powerfully defied this "hands-off" perspective the day He broke into our world as a babe laying in a manger. Even after this same Jesus accomplished the work of eternal salvation

*Pentecost was heaven's divine solution to an orphaned planet.*

on Calvary, God the Father ensured that His people would not be left on earth as orphans (see John 14:18).

Pentecost was heaven's divine solution to an orphaned planet, as we so clearly see in Acts 2. While we can all agree that the Holy

Spirit has been poured out upon all believers, the age-old debate is *what* the Holy Spirit actually empowers us to accomplish in this lifetime. May the pages ahead stir your heart to believe for more and equip you to step into every supernatural empowerment God has made available to you through His Spirit.

## Part One

# WHY IS THERE DIVISION OVER THE HOLY SPIRIT?

*When the day of Pentecost came, they were all together in one place. Suddenly a sound like the blowing of a violent wind came from heaven and filled the whole house where they were sitting. They saw what seemed to be tongues of fire that separated and came to rest on each of them. All of them were filled with the Holy Spirit and began to speak in other tongues as the Spirit enabled them.* —ACTS 2:1-4

When we look at Acts 2:1-4, and study the outpouring of the Holy Spirit at Pentecost, we should note that the tongues of fire *separated* and *came to rest on each* of those who were present in the upper room. Other translations have used the phrase "*divided tongues.*" Only in God's Kingdom can divided tongues be intended to produce unity—but this is one of the benefits that Pentecost was purposed to unlock: supernatural unity throughout the body of Christ that reveals Jesus to the world (see John 17:22-23).

Though Jesus had ascended into heaven before leaving Earth, He spoke of One coming who would be a glorious *advantage* to those who would receive Him. Read how Jesus was preparing the disciples to receive this advantage, the promised Holy Spirit:

*Nevertheless I tell you the truth. It is to your advantage that I go away; for if I do not go away, the Helper will not come to you; but if I depart, I will send Him to you.* (John 16:7 NKJV)

At that moment in time, the disciples' minds could not fathom the possibility of an advantage. They could not consider a reality greater than having Jesus physically present with them. And yet, Jesus Himself informed them that it was *"for your good that I am going away"* (John 16:7).

Even today, believers mistakenly long for "the good old days" or the "one day" of the future. We either wish we could have been among the disciples who were present during Jesus's time on earth, or we look forward to a future day when we will be able to visibly see Jesus in all of His glory, either in heaven, during the millennial reign, or whatever our theology dictates.

> There is controversy because there is truth that needs to be rediscovered.

Here is my question to you: What about today? What about now? This is why I believe this guide is essential. I want to help you navigate the importance of the Holy Spirit's power in your life today. There is controversy because there is truth that needs to be rediscovered.

The wrong approach is to see controversy as an invitation to disengage from the conversation entirely. No. While our call is not to angrily fire back at those who question the validity of the Spirit's power today, we must constructively search the Scriptures in order to navigate this debate for ourselves.

Remember, divided tongues were not given for the purpose of dividing the church. They produced a supernatural unity in the early church that changed the spiritual landscape of society. It was unity that prepared the disciples' hearts for the Spirit's coming on that day, as they all met in one accord (see Acts 2:1), and it is likewise unity that the Holy Spirit has come to produce in today's church. Paul exhorts us to endeavor *"to keep the unity of the Spirit"* (Eph. 4:3).

Before we begin our study of the controversy, however, I want us to approach this topic with great sensitivity. It is just as dangerous for us to become hypercritical as it is for us to remain ignorant—both approaches assault Christian unity. We are addressing the issues for one key purpose: to constructively advance in our Christian lives, operating in every grace, gift, and endowment that the supernatural power of the Holy Spirit scripturally offers us.

John 14–17 represents Jesus's farewell address to the disciples. In this context, He prepares them for what is to come—His death, but also the provision of the Holy Spirit. Consider these stirring words from the Savior as we press on toward unity in the Spirit and maximum effectiveness in advancing His Kingdom. As Jesus prays for all believers throughout all generations, He says to the Father:

> *And the glory which You gave Me I have given them, that they may be one just as We are one: I in them, and You in Me; that they may be made perfect in one, and that the world may know that You have sent Me, and have loved them as You have loved Me.* (John 17:22-23 NKJV)

The only one who makes this incredible reality possible, *Christ in you* and *Christ in me*, is the Holy Spirit. In order to live this out, let's do our best to wade through the controversies. Remember, controversy in the Kingdom is only attached to truths of vital importance. It goes without saying that the Holy Spirit, the third person of the Trinity, and the very member of the Godhead who has come to abide with us on earth, is certainly of the *most vital importance* for our lives today!

*Chapter 1*

# THE CONTINUING CONTROVERSY

*Understanding why there is still division attached
to the supernatural power of the Holy Spirit.*

## THE AGE-OLD CONTROVERSY

Cessationism is *not* a theology; it simply represents one approach to theology. Cessationism is a perspective that believes the movement of the Holy Spirit, particularly through the supernatural *sign gifts* (i.e., tongues, prophecy, and miracles, as listed in 1 Corinthians 12 and 14) have ceased. Therefore, they should no longer be expected or encouraged as normative practice for the contemporary New Testament church. On the other hand, continuationism is the belief that the gifts and power of the Holy Spirit have continued since the day of Pentecost and are relevant for Christians today.

Right from the start, I do not wish to paint with broad strokes. I do not consider all believers who embrace a cessationist perspective to be of "like mind" and approach. These are brothers and sisters in the faith, many of whom are significantly contributing to the advancement of the gospel across the earth. With heartfelt gratitude, I celebrate their roles in the Kingdom of God—in evangelism, apologetics, theological study, upholding the centrality of the cross, and other such exploits.

With that said, some of those who embrace the cessationist paradigm have become particularly outspoken throughout the centuries, denouncing modern expressions of supernatural power as false, counterfeit, and, even worse, demonic. Many of the voices throughout history fueled by this mission to denounce all forms of Charismatic expression tend to resort to the same old methodology and arguments. Their books are often difficult to read and their messages prove to be a challenge to hear without feeling slimed by false comparisons and an incomplete commitment to *sola Scriptura* (Scripture alone).

## THE IMBALANCED CESSATIONIST APPROACH

Some of the outspoken modern cessationists tend to ignore large parts of the Scriptures that are pertinent in order to give a fair biblical perspective on the issue of both offices and gifts of the Holy Spirit. These works often fall short of the biblical exegetical contributions of biblical theologians such as Jon Ruthven, in his two books on the subject, *What's Wrong with Protestant Theology? Tradition vs. Biblical Emphasis* and *On the Cessation of the Charismata: A Protestant Polemic on Post-biblical Miracles.*

These cessationist works also do not go into as much depth as the book by Dr. Gary Greig and Kevin Springer, *The Kingdom and the Power: Are Healing and the Spiritual Gifts Used by Jesus and the Early Church Meant for the Church Today?* or Craig Keener's *Miracles: The Credibility of the New Testament Accounts.*[1]

I believe that cessationists should be dealing with works like these if they truly want to be committed to sola Scriptura. While there are many notable theological and academic voices who embrace the cessationist perspective, there are also theological and academic voices who represent the other side of the argument. Unfortunately, their invaluable contributions are often not explored or even acknowledged.

Though many of the most vocal proponents of cessationism are Reformed in their theology, embracing the doctrines and perspectives of men such as Augustine and John Calvin, it is fascinating to note how both of these pioneers of Reformed thought exhibited an unusual openness to the supernatural power of the Holy Spirit.

## CALVIN AND OTHER HISTORIC LEADERS ON SIGNS, WONDERS, AND MIRACLES

Many Reformed cessationists fail to mention that John Calvin's approach to the charismata was not one of complete withdrawal. According to church historian Dr. Vinson Synan, Calvin maintained a unique perspective on the gifts of the Holy Spirit, explaining "that they (the gifts) fell into disuse in the churches because of a 'lack of faith.'"[2] Calvin "never forbade their use or felt that they should be forbidden. Moreover, because of his extended attention to the Third Person of the Trinity in his writings, he has been called the 'theologian of the Holy Spirit' among reformers."[3]

> *Many of the early church fathers acknowledged the possibility of the continuing work of the Holy Spirit.*

Thus, Calvin is *not* strictly adhering to a classical, pure cessationist perspective that completely disregards the possibility of post-apostolic demonstrations of supernatural power. In fact, many of the early church fathers acknowledged the possibility of the continuing work of the Holy Spirit. Going a step further, several of these men and women actually experienced the Spirit's power for themselves.

John Huss believed that dreams are a means of supernatural communication from God. The Bohemian Brethren experienced signs and wonders through the middle of the sixteenth century.[4] Martin Luther himself believed in the continued power of prayer to deliver people who were demonized and prayer's effectiveness to heal the sick.[5] He prayed to heal both Philipp Melanchthon and Friedrich Myconius,[6] both of whom were healed from death's door through Luther's prayers. Luther also spoke by the Spirit what Charismatics today would call prophecies, and many of them were fulfilled.[7] Johannes Mathesius, one of Luther's earliest biographers, wrote that "with many sure prophecies he confirmed his doctrine."[8]

History reveals that the Scottish Covenanters and John Knox experienced gifts of the Holy Spirit as well.[9] I have outlined many other historical figures and movements who have embraced the power of the Holy Spirit in my books *There Is More!*[10] and *The Essential Guide to Healing.*[11]

## THROWING THE GOOD AND THE BAD TOGETHER

The cessationist method in general seems to use many negative adjectives against the opposing position and continually indicates that any opposing positions are wrong. As in many past works on the subject of cessationism, and in B. B. Warfield's classic *Counterfeit Miracles*, there is a continued use of creating a composite *straw man* that is made up of the most embarrassing examples of the Pentecostal, Charismatic, and Third Wave positions. Many cessationists incorrectly refer to this composite as the *Charismatic Movement.*

The same logic motivating this blanket approach would thereby take a fringe, but nevertheless vocal, example of "Christianity," such as the Westboro Baptist Church, and assume that their actions are characteristic of the entire Baptist Movement as a whole. Of course, this line of thought is utterly preposterous. Sadly, many highly-educated and learned individuals use this method of faulty evaluation in making broad, all-encompassing statements concerning the Charismatic Movement in its entirety.

The Charismatic Movement caricature is then attacked, and attempts are made to discredit this composite group of Pentecostals, Charismatics, and Third Wave Evangelicals.[12] Rather than argue from biblical exegesis, some cessationists prefer the *ad hominem* argument, "against the man." This strategy seems to place the best of the teaching in the movement and the most balanced positions within the movement side by side with the weakest and poorest examples—both morally and exegetically. This discrediting of the *witness* (a witness made up of both authentic and abhorrent expressions of the Charismatic Movement), is supposed to discredit the entire Pentecostal, Charismatic, and Third Wave Movements.

## NOT ALL MOVEMENTS ARE CREATED EQUAL

Truth be told, there is great diversity between the three movements listed above. As one studies each group with increased precision and care, they will note that there is even great diversity *within* each of the three aforementioned Charismatic groups. However, the one common denominator is that all believe in the continuation of the gifts of the Spirit in the church today. The very person who was sent from heaven to preserve Christian unity has sadly become a source of great division to many in the body of Christ.

The attacks on this caricature, the Charismatic *straw man*, tend to be vicious assaults, without love for Christian brothers and sisters, even questioning whether or not they are Christians to begin with. It seems that the purpose is often not to systematically deal with the true scholarly arguments of defenders of continuationism, but rather to assign fear to one's perception of Charismatic demonstrations and expressions.

> *The very person who was sent from heaven to preserve Christian unity has sadly become a source of great division to many in the body of Christ.*

Earlier I introduced you to the reality of multiple kinds of cessationists. Just as all Charismatics are not created equal, likewise, not all cessationists take up residence in the "same camp." In several cases, we are able to theologically disagree on the continuation of the Holy Spirit's gifts and yet live amicably as fellow brothers and sisters in the expansion of the gospel. We might even collaborate together on different ministry projects or initiatives.

Sadly, there are others in the body of Christ who take this issue beyond a theological debate or a topic of disagreement. They seem to be aimed at creating an emotional response of suspicion and fear in regards to those who embrace the continuationist position. In other words, they paint a picture of the Charismatic Movement as an unsettling, unorthodox, and anti-Christian expression. This is dangerous to the curious believers who are hungry to make proper, biblical sense of the continuationist perspective, but most of all it jeopardizes the possibility of enjoying unity in the body of Christ.

In the same manner that I, as one voice representative of the Charismatic Movement, desire a fair and balanced treatment of our nuances, I likewise wish to extend this same courtesy toward those who embrace a cessationist perspective.

The controversy I have been describing in previous paragraphs has been generated by cessationists who not only disagree with the present move of the Holy Spirit's power, but who consistently hurl attacks at believers who adhere to a continuationist point of view. This discourages unity in the body of Christ and is completely counterproductive to our global mandate to proclaim the gospel. I suggest that we tone down our attacks and endeavor to work through these vital topics as Christian brothers and sisters who love God's Word and embrace His Spirit.

## Summary

In order to start operating in the power of the Holy Spirit, it is important for all believers to navigate through the controversies, understand the arguments at hand, and take an uncompromised stand for the truth.

## Power Points

1. **Cessationism:** A point of view that considers the sign gifts of the Holy Spirit (as identified in 1 Corinthians 12 and 14: tongues, prophecy, working of miracles) as having ceased after the close of the initial apostolic age, or the canonization of the Bible.

2. **Continuationism:** A point of view that embraces the continuation of the sign gifts and supernatural power of the Holy Spirit, from the day of Pentecost until the consummation of the age at Jesus's return.

3. Just because there are abuses, misuses, and theological errors circulating in the Charismatic Movement,

it is irresponsible for us to disregard an entire movement—or worse, brand everyone within the larger
movement as a heretic—because of the errors propagated by some.

4. Even though we may differ on theological viewpoints,
   it is essential for us to maintain an attitude of love
   and Christian unity as we debate and dialogue about
   the issues.

*Chapter 2*

# WHAT ARE THE PROBLEMS WITH POWER?

*Exploring some of the most popular Charismatic controversies
and upholding God's ultimate standard: Scripture.*

## STEP BACK AND SEE DIFFERENTLY

When it comes to reviewing the power of the Holy Spirit in action, we cannot afford to simply observe all Charismatic activity as being "created equal." In other words, not everything said or done in the name of the Holy Spirit is an accurate representation of His nature or power. Throughout our time together, I want us to seriously consider some of the issues that have plagued the Charismatic Movement and tend to add fuel to the fire of controversy for many.

However, to appropriately sort through these topics in a constructive manner, it is important for us to take a few steps back. Regardless of what perspective you have adopted on the Charismatic Movement as a whole, I want to encourage you to move away from the popular perspective of branding *all things* Charismatic as one and the same. We tackled this approach briefly in the previous chapter, but it bears repeating here—especially as we are getting ready to wade through some of the most popular points of the controversy and contention.

> *Not everything said or done in the name of the Holy Spirit is an accurate representation of His nature or power.*

A common cessationist way of arguing would be to include the farthest-right dispensational fundamentalists and farthest-left liberals in the Evangelical Movement, all linked together because they do not believe in the continuation of the gifts of the Holy Spirit today. Within this contrived composite *straw man* representing evangelicalism, one could find many embarrassing examples of moral failure, theological error, and financial impropriety. Quotes could be found that would appear from ridiculous to heretical, especially if the extremes of the far-right fundamentalist and the far-left liberal movements were analyzed.

As my purpose is to respond to some of the common controversies surrounding the Charismatic Movement, I do not wish to practice a similar willingness to attack fellow Christians. The goal is to inform you, but also to provide a constructive outlet for thoughtful reconsideration. I am merely pointing out that in creating a composite *straw man* from such divergent groups, one is able to find many examples that are not good representations of the movement as a whole.

That said, I believe it is best for us to represent a movement by its best and not its worst examples of theological correctness and moral holiness. This is important to keep in mind as we get ready to honestly examine some of the key issues of controversy within the Charismatic Movement.

# LACK OF BIBLICAL DISCERNMENT AND SOLID SCHOLARSHIP

The Charismatic Movement has long been accused of relying on experience over Scripture. While this erroneous perspective may be representative for some Charismatics, it is by no means the case for all. The Bible gives clear tests for discerning whether something is from God or if is false. There is not just *one* test; rather, there are several.

There is the primary test to which Jesus allluded: the test of the fruit:

> *Jesus answered, "My teaching is not My own. It comes from Him who sent Me. If anyone chooses to do God's will, he will find out whether My teaching comes from God or whether I speak on My own." (John 7:16-17)*

There is also the text of affirming or denying the incarnation:

> *Dear friends, do not believe every spirit, but test the spirits to see whether they are from God, because many false prophets have gone out into the world. This is how you can recognize the Spirit of God: Every spirit that acknowledges that Jesus Christ has come in the flesh is from God, but every spirit that does not acknowledge Jesus is not from God. This is the spirit of the antichrist, which you have heard is coming and even now is already in the world. (1 John 4:1-3)*

There is the test of denying the importance of the historical Jesus and attributing such declarations to the Holy Spirit:

> *Therefore I tell you that no one who is speaking by the Spirit of God says, "Jesus be cursed," and no one can say,*

THE ESSENTIAL GUIDE TO THE POWER OF THE HOLY SPIRIT

*"Jesus is Lord," except by the Holy Spirit.* (1 Corinthians 12:3)

There is the test of worship, which is the test given in the book of Revelation: will we worship the Lamb or the beast?

*All inhabitants of the earth will worship the beast—all whose names have not been written in the book of life belonging to the Lamb that was slain from the creation of the world.* (Revelation 13:8)

The lying signs and wonders of 1 Thessalonians 2:8-10, Matthew 24:24, and the book of Revelation, serve the purpose of causing people to turn from Jesus Christ to worship another, whether the man of lawlessness, the antichrist, or the beast or his false prophet.

This mode of evaluation should cause us to look at *non-Christians*, not at groups that place a high priority on worshiping the Triune God. Who focuses on healing but denies the incarnation, the lordship of Jesus, and believes that His earthly life is not important? Who believes the "christ spirit" that was not only upon Jesus but also upon Buddha, Mohammad, Zoroaster, and continues to come in the form of other Avatars? It is not Pentecostals, Charismatics, and Third Wavers, but rather those who ascribe to New Age philosophy and false religion.

It is likewise erroneous to assume that no valid scholarship has been achieved among the Charismatic community or, even worse, that there are no Charismatic scholars, academics, or leaders contributing to the furtherance of theological study. Such a deduction would be very misleading. Instead of highlighting those who have fallen into doctrinal error, why not note the honorable, theologically well-balanced leaders like the Roman Catholic Dr. Francis

MacNutt, the Anglican Bishop David Pytches, the Foursquare Pentecostal Dr. Jack Hayford, or the distinguished Methodist professors of United Theological Seminary, Dr. Peter Bellini, Dr. Luther Oconer, or Dr. Andrew Park?

One could also mention the Calvinist, Dr. R. T. Kendall, the former professors of Regent University Divinity School, Dr. Jon Ruthven and Dr. Gary Greig, and the highly respected Charismatic Baptist New Testament scholar of Asbury Theological Seminary, Dr. Craig Keener, whose two-volume work *Miracles* was required reading in my doctoral class.

> *Scripture is not simply a book to be read and studied, but it is an invitation into a lifestyle of supernatural engagement.*

One could argue that it is actually the Pentecostals, Charismatics, and Third Wavers who are taking the Bible more seriously than even some cessationists, making it not only the source for their theology, but also the source for their practices. For many Charismatics, Scripture is not simply a book to be read and studied, but it is an invitation into a lifestyle of supernatural engagement. Truly, such followers of Jesus desire to be doers of the Word, not hearers only. This should be celebrated rather than rejected.

## THE PROSPERITY GOSPEL

One of the most frequent examples of this Charismatic caricature or *straw man* is in reference to the prosperity gospel. While this is certainly an embarrassing problem that has plagued the Charismatic Movement for decades, one cannot simply assume that anyone who believes in the modern demonstration of the Holy Spirit's power also embraces the insidious prosperity gospel.

Critics and cessationist leaders have rightfully addressed the overemphasis upon material prosperity. What seems unbalanced in their arguments is the total failure to acknowledge the self-corrective attempts to address this very issue from within the Word of Faith Movement.

Word of Faith is only a part of the Charismatic Movement. It by no means represents the vast majority of Pentecostals, Charismatics, and Third Wavers or other continuationists. Many fail to note that Kenneth Hagin's last book, and one of his last conferences for the Word of Faith Movement, was *The Midas Touch*, which was Hagin's attempt to call the movement to a balanced position of not overemphasizing material prosperity at the expense of spiritual prosperity.[13]

When it comes to the issue of the prosperity gospel, we cannot follow the "guilty by association" approach. It is important to recognize that the Word of Faith Movement is about much more than just material prosperity. In the same way that a single example of Charismatic abuse cannot speak representatively on behalf of the entire movement, let alone its myriad of expressions and diversities, likewise, the grievous errors that have accompanied *prosperity preaching* should not be applied to all adherents of the Word of Faith Movement.

Accusations have been made that the majority of Nigerian Christians, along with the vast percentage of believers in the Philippines, believe that God will grant good health and relief from sickness to those who have enough faith. Many would mistakenly assume that these same Christians are also proponents of the prosperity gospel simply because they believe in divine healing received through faith.

The fact is that divine healing has been and continues to be a main doctrine of Pentecostals, Charismatics, and Third Wavers throughout the world. This is a true statement, but to extrapolate that if one believes in the benefits of healing through the cross, then one also embraces the prosperity gospel, especially in its extreme form, is a false deduction.

Personally speaking as one of the members of the Revival Alliance—which is made up of six networks that would fall into the Pentecostal, Charismatic, or Third Wave category—there is among us an understanding of blessings and curses related to covenant lifestyles. However, there is a majority opinion that this message is not to be perverted by focusing on the overtly material aspect of this truth, to the point that our goal becomes the building of our personal kingdom instead of His Kingdom. Our focus is on being blessed to give, not what kind of car we drive, how large our homes are, or what kind of jewelry or watches we wear. Claims such as "Jesus was rich" seem ludicrous in light of scriptural evidence. High-powered, guilt-ridden offerings are discouraged, and giving in order to get rich to spend money on ourselves is frowned upon.

Also, I believe that the majority of Pentecostal churches in America today would not embrace the prosperity gospel in its extreme nature either. Just because one adheres to a certain Charismatic teaching, namely, the continuing availability of the Holy Spirit's miraculous power for today, does not automatically mean that this same individual embraces any variation of the "prosperity gospel."

## WORD OF FAITH/POSITIVE CONFESSION

Many have tried to connect the Word of Faith Movement, particularly the teachings of E. W. Kenyon, to the *New Thought Movement* emerging out of New England. Likewise, many evangelicals—including some Pentecostals—have characterized Kenyon as one with roots in New Thought, leaning more toward New Age philosophy than historic orthodoxy.

However, others have proven that New Thought did not influence Kenyon at all. Rather, his true source of influence was the Holiness Movement, especially the Keswick Movement, and the greatest influence upon E. W. Kenyon was A. J. Gordon, the Baptist, after whom Gordon-Conwell Seminary is named.[14]

## MORAL FAILURE OF KEY CHARISMATIC LEADERS

Critics tend to parade the failure of well-known leaders of the Charismatic Movement, using their personal tragedies as examples of the alleged unbiblical nature of the movement as a whole. However, the conclusion that there is less moral failure among evangelical leaders than among Charismatics remains to be proven.

While I was in seminary, one of the professors fell into sexual sin and divorced his wife. A leading evangelical Bible teacher on the radio also did the same. Moral failures occur within all groups of Christendom. I am sad for any leader who falls due to a moral failure. Such incidents are undeniably tragic, and we would do well to pray for the individuals who fell into grievous sin, for their families who were severely affected, and those who have been influenced by their ministries.

At the same time, it would be irresponsible from this to deduct that all evangelical seminary professors or evangelical radio Bible teachers are like the two examples I just listed. In like manner, there are thousands of leaders in the Charismatic Movement who live lives of purity and holiness.[15] All over the world there are people in this movement who are laid down lovers of Jesus Christ, who are being spent on His call, and who are spending their own wealth to advance the gospel of the Kingdom of God.

*Heidi and Rolland Baker—Iris Ministries.* Drs. Heidi and Rolland Baker (Iris Ministries), in Mozambique, are two of the most radical people of faith I know, and they have seen one million people come to Jesus through their ministry. They understand that the gospel includes presence evangelism, presentation evangelism, and power evangelism.[16]

> *The gospel includes presence evangelism, presentation evangelism, and power evangelism.*

They are involved in well drilling, food production, micro-businesses, feeding and clothing programs, as well as preaching the gospel, calling for repentance and commitment to Christ. This is accompanied by healings, miracles, and the dead being raised, which have turned entire Muslim provinces into Christian provinces in the nation of Mozambique. The good fruit of Iris Ministries is undeniable and far-reaching.

*Carlos Annacondia.* In the Western Hemisphere, there is Carlos Annacondia—a wealthy businessman who serves the poor, conducting crusades at his own expense. Annacondia has led scores of thousands to the Lord, one time more than 50,000 and at another time about 80,000, through crusades in Argentina. These crusades have seen approximately 80 percent of the new converts become part of the church, unlike our North American crusades where only 6 percent of the ones who go forward for prayer end up in a church.

*Everyday "Little Ole Mes."* Then there are the nameless, faceless, "little ole mes" who travel on ministry teams all over the world with Global Awakening. They pay their own way, receive nothing for their service of prayer for healing and deliverance, and use their personal vacation time to travel. Usually up to 50 percent of the thousands who are healed during the Global Awakening trips are healed not from the platform prayers of the speaker, but from this army of lovers of Jesus Christ, who believe in the gifts of healing, and who witness His power flow through them touching the indigenous people.

To get an accurate understanding of Charismatic theology, it is not to our benefit to draw upon some of the worst aspects in the character of some of the founders of the Pentecostal and Charismatic Movements. As regrettable as some of these behaviors are, this does not prove the movement is false any more than one could point to the strong anti-Semitic statements of Martin Luther, the drowning of the Anabaptists by Lutherans, the burning of Servetus by John Calvin in Switzerland, or the early rejection of missions by most Protestants.

In the same way that it would be unwise for us to make wholesale assumptions about Reformed theology solely based on the grievous actions of the aforementioned pioneers and leaders, it is unwise for us to apply the same measuring stick to the Charismatic Movement. This is not a call for us to excuse negative behavior, sinful actions, and theological heresy.

Consider this: If the worst statements and conduct by all non-Pentecostals and Charismatics were to be marshaled against Protestantism as a wholesale movement, it would not be a fair characterization of Protestantism. The same could be said for Roman Catholicism. The fallible character of some of the founders of Protestantism, the effect of cultural bias and prejudice, and theological prejudice do not invalidate the spiritual truths of these respective movements. They merely prove that God often uses people with brokenness, people who are sinners saved by grace.

## "Tokin' the Ghost"

Some of most embarrassing examples of a lack of wisdom on the part of some young Charismatic leaders include the practice of "tokin' the Ghost," where the Holy Spirit is treated liked a drug.

Many reputable Charismatic leaders are unwilling to endorse a particular young minister due to this language. In fact, I pulled one of my spiritual sons, a prophetic minister himself, aside and warned him of the lack of wisdom of such a practice. He only used this language once and immediately heeded my cautionary warning.

While not at all defending the excesses or the extremes of the Charismatic Movement, it is worth remembering that the manifestations of extremes in some Charismatic services should not be allowed to thereby condemn all Charismatic services as also embracing the bizarre manifestations.

## IT IS TIME TO CHALLENGE AND CHANGE OUR ARGUMENTS

What if I, having spent fourteen years as a pastor in evangelical churches, told you the true stories of people falling asleep in church, disrupting the service by their snoring, and made the implication that this was typical of *all* evangelical worship services? What if I told you the true story of an angry Baptist who came to my church with a shotgun, unwilling to let anyone enter the building, and then proceeded to imply that this was typical of an evangelical worship service?

Or I could mention my experience in another evangelical church where some of the members publicly spoke out about how evil their stepmother had been, and how they would never forgive her. What made this incident even worse was that the stepmother was a practicing member of the *same* church. I could also recount the true story of attending another evangelical church that, by the time I was twelve, had split *four times* due to infighting.

Writing about such true experiences would cause the less discerning to deduct that *those evangelicals* are so lethargic in their worship toward God that they fall asleep in church, they are angry, unforgiving, and dangerous to be around.

This would be an unfair caricature of the evangelical church, in the same way as the previously discussed abnormalities should be regarded as unfair representatives of the Charismatic Movement as a whole.

## Summary

Just because there are imbalances and extremes observable in the Charismatic Movement—all of which should be taken seriously by leaders and adherents—this does not give one legitimate, scriptural grounds to discredit the availability of the Holy Spirit's power for today.

## Power Points

1. Step back and see the Charismatic Movement differently, defining both belief and practice by the standard of Scripture, not fringe doctrines and fallen leaders.

2. Boldly confront the abuses and imbalances while recognizing that the worst examples of a movement should never represent the movement as a whole.

3. Ensure that the ultimate standard by which we understand the Holy Spirit's power is what Scripture clearly reveals as truth.

# Chapter 3

# TRACING THE HOLY SPIRIT'S POWERFUL HAND IN HISTORY

*Discovering how the Holy Spirit has been powerfully and actively at work in the world since the day of Pentecost.*

History demands a careful second glance when it comes to tracing the continuation of the Holy Spirit's power since Pentecost. As mentioned in chapter 1, some of the key figures used by many cessationists as hallmarks of those who refute or reject the Holy Spirit's power are, in actuality, those who experienced it in dramatic ways.

## AUGUSTINE

One of the most notable examples is St. Augustine of Hippo. Cessationists often neglect to inform us that Augustine believed people were still being baptized in the Holy Spirit during their water baptism and through the laying on of hands. However, he did not believe that it was happening to all.

He also believed that speaking in tongues was sometimes still happening at this occasion. In fact, Augustine had much to say about the baptism in the Holy Spirit and the charisms of the Spirit. In relationship to water baptism, he stated: "We must not think that those who have received a valid (water) baptism have also automatically (*continuo*) received the Holy Spirit."[17] Augustine's quote, in context, is referring to the baptism in the Holy Spirit.

Closer to the end of his life, Augustine wrote retractions in which he mentions seventy healings that took place in just two years in his bishopric, and that other bishops were also aware of healing in their bishoprics.[18] It has also been discovered that Augustine himself developed a healing ministry and a deliverance ministry.[19]

## THE EARLY CHURCH

History unveils that during the first few hundred years of the church, when one was baptized, manifestations of gifts of the Spirit, including speaking in tongues, accompanied the water baptisms of adults coming out of paganism in the missionary expansion of the church.

Tertullian instructed catechumens preparing for baptism,

> Therefore, you blessed ones, for whom the grace of God is waiting, when you come up from the most sacred bath of the new birth, when you spread out your hands for the first time in your mother's house with your brethren, ask your Father, ask your Lord, for the special gift of His inheritance, the distributed charisms [gifts of the Holy Spirit].... Ask, He says, and you shall receive.[20]

# FAMOUS REFORMED LEADERS, PREACHERS, AND PASTORS

Even though cessationists often cite the works of theologians who embrace a Reformed perspective, there is nevertheless a compelling body of evidence suggesting that the very individuals who are used to lend credibility to a cessationist perspective have personally encountered the power of the Holy Spirit through "Charismatic experiences."

Interestingly enough, notable preacher and pastor, Charles Spurgeon, was known for his ministry of healing prayer.[21] In fact, sometimes during Spurgeon's sermons he would give information about someone's sin that today in the Charismatic Movement would be considered a "word of knowledge."

We cannot ignore the accounts of early Scottish reformers during the time of John Knox in Scotland who experienced the gift of prophecy.[22] Finally, there are several historical accounts of reformers experiencing what Charismatics today would call the gifts of healing, discerning of spirits, prophecy, and words of knowledge.

## THE POWER FALLS THROUGHOUT REVIVAL HISTORY

One notable pastor once questioned, "Does the Holy Spirit really cause people to fall down like bowling pins?" The answer is yes. The truth is that many of the manifestations that are often vilified, like the one mentioned above, did happen in the Bible, and throughout the history of revivals.[23] It is also true that powerful encounters with the Holy Spirit, which are sometimes marked by some of the manifestations ridiculed and mocked by critics, result in the very things one considers to be "lasting fruit."

45

As we continue this brief exploration throughout history, we see that this particular manifestation occurred quite often in periods of revival. This phenomenon occurred during the First Great Awakening, the Second Great Awakening, under the ministry of Charles Finney, and the missionary C. T. Studd, who was one of the Cambridge Seven and who responded to Hudson Taylor's call for missionaries, as well as many more.

> *Powerful encounters with the Holy Spirit, which are sometimes marked by some of the manifestations ridiculed and mocked by critics, result in the very things one considers to be "lasting fruit."*

Though manifestations, such as falling "under the power" of the Holy Spirit, have been considered controversial, theologians confirm their presence throughout the halls of Scripture. Dr. Gary Greig catalogues the manifestations and phenomenon of the Bible as follows, and the presence of God's Spirit in power and glory may be marked in Scripture by the following references:

- *Shaking or trembling*—Exodus 19:16; 1 Chronicles 16:30; Ezra 9:4; Psalm 2:11; 96:9; 114:7; 119:120; Isaiah 66:5; Jeremiah 5:22, 23:9; Daniel 10:10-11; Matthew 28:4; Acts 7:32; Hebrews 12:21.

- *Falling over*—Genesis 17:3; 1 Kings 8:11; Ezekiel 1:28, 3:23; Daniel 8:17-18, 10:9; John 18:6; Acts 9:4; 26:14; 1 Corinthians 14:25; Revelation 1:17.

- *Intoxicated state of mind*—Acts 2:4, 13, 15; Ephesians 5:18; cf. 1 Samuel 1:12-17; 19:23.

- *Bodily writhing and distortion under the influence of a demon*—Mark 1:21-26; 9:26; Luke 8:28.

- *Laughing, shouting, or weeping*—Genesis 17:17;[24] Ezra 3:13 ("rejoicing," which certainly included laughter and shouting, is so loud that it is heard "far away" from Jerusalem—that must have been pretty loud!); Nehemiah 8:6, 9 (weeping in the midst of worship and praise), 12:43; Psalm 126:2; Proverbs 14:13; Acts 14:10 (Greek literally "[Paul] *said with a loud voice*").

- *Prolonged exuberant praise*—Luke 1:41-42 (Elizabeth, "filled with the Holy Spirit, spoke out in a loud voice"), 46-55, 64, 68-79; 5:25; 17:15; Acts 3:8-10.

- *Feeling energy, electricity, or heat*—Mark 5:29-30 (see also Matthew 9:22; Luke 8:44, 46-47); Luke 6:19; cf. Colossians 1:29 (where *energeia*, "working, energy"[25] is coupled in the text with *dunamis* "power"); Judges 14:6, 19, 15:14; 1 Samuel 10:6, 10:10.[26]

- *Feeling deep peace*—Romans 14:17; 15:13; 1 Corinthians 14:33; Philippians 4:5-7.

- *Visible radiance seen on the face or around the head*—Acts 2:3-4 (tongues of fire); 6:15; 7:55 (Stephen filled with the Spirit had a radiant face);[27] and compare that with 2 Corinthians 3:7, 13, 17-18 and Exodus 34:29 (the radiance of Moses face is from the "*Lord who is the Spirit*").

- *Trance-like state*—Acts 10:10; 22:17.

■ *Groaning or inarticulate sounds*—Romans 8:26.

These phenomena, which may accompany the presence of God's Spirit, are not only attested to in Scripture, but they are also attested to in early Judaism[28] and early, post-biblical Christian tradition.

## BIBLICAL EXAMPLE: DANIEL PHYSICALLY RESPONDS TO THE POWER OF GOD

Though some would argue against the historical revival accounts—claiming that simply because certain phenomena have been experienced does not verify their scriptural validity—one cannot escape examples in the Bible where notable figures physically experienced and reacted to the power of God.

> *One cannot escape examples in the Bible where notable figures physically experienced and reacted to the power of God.*

The Bible records manifestations such as Daniel's experience (see Dan. 10:7-11), where he lost his strength, trembled, and fell to the ground. Though Daniel did not use the word *electricity*, for those who have a very strong sensation of trembling, it is often due to the feeling of energy or electricity in their bodies.

Almost all the passages in the Old Testament that mention trembling do so in the context of fear, fear and trembling, or trembling due to fear. However, Daniel 10:10 seems to be an exception where the trembling is not out of fear, but due to the power of God entering Daniel when he was touched. Daniel 10:10-11 reads,

*A hand touched me and set me trembling on my hands and knees. He said, "Daniel, you who are highly esteemed, consider carefully the words I am about to speak to you, and stand up, for I have now been sent to you." And when He said this to me, I stood up trembling.*

The accusation that the apostles were drunk on the day of Pentecost is indicative of behavior similar to manifestations someone would have if under the strong influence of alcohol. And the apostle Paul spoke of laboring with all of God's energy that worked so mightily within him.[29]

It simply is not true that the Bible has no mention of trembling, falling, joy, drunkenness in the Spirit, or energy. In fact, both the Old and New Testaments contain several examples of people being touched by the power of God and responding in unusual ways. This must be our standard if we are to fully embrace the Spirit's renewing work in our midst today.

## Summary

The Holy Spirit's power is not the invention of a movement, denomination, or specific century. He has been active in the earth since Genesis 1, and history makes it clear that notable Christian leaders, pioneers, and forerunners have had dramatic, transformative experiences with His supernatural presence.

## Power Principles

1. History and Scripture are filled with examples of experiencing the Holy Spirit's power in dramatic, unusual ways.

2.  The Bible is our ultimate source for the validity of revival manifestations.

3.  We cannot discredit a manifestation of the Spirit's power and presence in someone's life simply because we find its expression uncomfortable.

4.  Regardless of our personal preferences or denominational backgrounds, we must be open to receive the powerful work of the Holy Spirit in our midst, as He is the only One who can transform a life and prepare a heart to receive the gospel.

## Part Two

# UNLOCKING THE GIFTS OF THE SPIRIT FOR TODAY

*Now to each one the manifestation of the Spirit is given for the common good. To one there is given through the Spirit the message of wisdom, to another the message of knowledge by means of the same Spirit, to another faith by the same Spirit, to another gifts of healing by that one Spirit, to another miraculous powers, to another prophecy, to another distinguishing between spirits, to another speaking in different kinds of tongues, and to still another the interpretation of tongues. All these are the work of one and the same Spirit, and He gives them to each one, just as He determines. —*I CORINTHIANS 12:7-11

*It was He who gave some to be apostles, some to be prophets, some to be evangelists, and some to be pastors and teachers, to prepare God's people for works of service, so that the body of Christ may be built up. —*EPHESIANS 4:11-12

In the following section, we are going to closely examine four of the most controversial demonstrations of the Holy Spirit's power. Two of these are manifestation gifts of the Holy Spirit, as listed by Paul in 1 Corinthians 12 and 14; and two of these are ministry offices, which Paul lists in Ephesians 4.

## MY PERSONAL EXPERIENCE WITH THE SIGN GIFTS

When it comes to the gifts of the Holy Spirit, as listed in 1 Corinthians 12, cessationists specifically maintain that the *sign gifts* have passed away. The very designation, *sign gifts,* is an extra-biblical designation not found in the text. These would include the more demonstrative, supernatural manifestations of the Holy Spirit, such as speaking in tongues and the working of miracles.

While I was working on my Master of Divinity degree at the Southern Baptist Theological Seminary in Louisville, Kentucky, almost forty years ago, I was taught that the purpose of tongues in the book of Acts was to correct the prejudiced Jewish leadership of the church. Tongues were seen as a sign, enabling the apostles to realize that God was breaking through religious and racial barriers to expand the inclusion of the church, moving from Jewish to Samaritans (half-Jews), to Gentile God-fearers who had joined themselves to the synagogues but had not become complete Jews because they had not been circumcised, to the Gentiles who were not God-fearers and were totally pagan.

If this was true, then it would be highly probable that the modern tongues movement, especially the Charismatic Movement, could be the work of the Holy Spirit attempting to reveal the unity of His church, and that it is much larger than some think.

It is very difficult for some Pentecostals to accept—that wine-drinking Catholics, beer-drinking Lutherans, and scotch-drinking Presbyterians were actually being baptized with the Holy Spirit.[30] It was hard for much of the church to accept the Jesus Movement of the '60s as a true move of God due to the people group He was saving—the hippies and the young of many nations.

I do not see ecumenism based upon the common experience of the Spirit to be unbiblical. In fact, it is this most unique experience of the Spirit that caused the apostolic church to accept the validity of Peter's experience at Cornelius's house in Acts 10–11.

## SIGNS OF INCREASING UNITY

The supernatural gifts that are under the most severe attack today—namely, speaking in tongues and divine healing—are two of the very gifts that have become embraced by groups within nearly every denomination. It seems as though the Holy Spirit has truly been no respecter of denominations, as Catholics (Kevin Ranaghan), Episcopalians (Dennis Bennett), and Lutherans (Larry Christenson) have embraced His gifts. Dr. Vinson Syn-an's book *The Century of the Holy Spirit* specifically catalogues each denomination that has been touched by the renewing power of the Spirit.

> *Could it be that, in spite of our doctrinal differences, the One who was sent from the Father is working to unite the body of Christ around what is most important?*

Instead of observing the Holy Spirit's power as a dividing agent, we should honestly evaluate the supernatural fruit His renewing work has produced in the church as a whole, both Protestant and Catholic. Could it be that, in spite of our doctrinal differences, the One who was sent from the Father is working to unite the body of Christ around what is most important?

# SIGNS THAT ACCOMPANY THE GOSPEL

I do not propose that sign gifts, healings, tongues, miracles, apostles, prophets, and demonstrations of power are the central rallying points around which the church should assemble. This is not a call to inappropriately exalt the Spirit's power, but to consider its purpose and the fruit it has been producing across the denominational spectrum. By and large, the Spirit's empowerment has not become a source of distraction for the different denominational churches who have embraced His work, but rather an integral focal point reminding us of the task we have all been anointed to complete—the Great Commission.

As we review the sign gifts of the Spirit—tongues and healing—along with the controversial offices of prophet and apostle, we would do well to consider them from a true evangelical point of view. Not *evangelical* in terms of a particular bent of Protestant theology, but rather in terms of the glorious *evangel* that Jesus instructed His followers to preach globally.

Evangelist Reinhard Bonnke said it well when he expressed that the gifts of the Spirit are not badges of honor; they are tools for the job. What is our job then? Jesus said, *"Go ye into all the world, and preach the gospel to every creature"* (Mark 16:15 KJV). It is actually in the context of preaching the gospel that we can begin to expect that these signs shall follow them that believe (see Mark 16:17).

# Chapter 4

# PROPHETS AND PROPHECY TODAY

*How God speaks to and through His people today.*

*It was [Christ] who gave some to be apostles, some to be
prophets, some to be evangelists, and some to be pastors
and teachers, to prepare God's people for works of service,
so that the body of Christ may be built up until we all
reach unity in the faith and in the knowledge of the
Son of God and become mature, attaining to the whole
measure of the fullness of Christ.* —EPHESIANS 4:11-13

Paul clearly states that the prophetic office will be utilized "until we
all reach unity in the faith and in the knowledge of the Son of God
and become mature, attaining to the whole measure of the fullness
of Christ" (Eph. 4:13). We have not entered into this unity, maturity,
and fullness yet, which means that until this is achieved, the body
of Christ will need the prophetic office—as well as the other four
offices listed in Ephesians 4:11-13.

## JUDGING PROPHECY

One of the reasons that prophecy tends to be rejected today, and
quickly branded as "false," is because many use an Old Testament

paradigm to evaluate the New Testament prophetic expression. We cannot use the Old Testament standard for prophecy instead of the New Testament standard. When we apply an Old Testament standard for judging prophecy, we tend to use a threefold test to find a false prophet, looking at 1) if the prophet's prophecies lead to false doctrine or heresy; 2) if the prophet lives in unrestrained lust or unrepentant sin; and 3) if someone who declares himself a prophet prophesies any alleged "revelation from God" that ends up being false, inaccurate, or untrue.

It is this evidential position for miracles, including prophecy, that some bring to their study of the biblical text that causes them to miss the true biblical purpose of both miracles and prophecy. As Dr. Jon Ruthven writes, they confuse "the sufficiency of revelation, i.e., in the unique historical manifestation of Christ and essential Christian doctrine, with the ongoing means of communicating, applying and actualizing that revelation, i.e., via such charismata as prophecy and miracles."[31] Ruthven continues, "The charismata do not so much accredit the Gospel as they express and concretize the Gospel."[32]

> *One of the reasons that prophecy tends to be rejected today, and quickly branded as "false," is because many use an Old Testament paradigm to evaluate the New Testament prophetic expression.*

By and large, those who embrace the validity of modern prophetic ministry and the pursuit of *revelation* are not seeking anything that would be considered "added" to Scripture. Revelation, often accompanying the prophetic ministry, is about us enhancing our clarity of what is *already* recorded in Scripture. I would agree with those who express disdain for any practice that involves seeking information that is beyond what we have been given through the recorded biblical narrative.

## PROPHECIES THAT DO NOT COME TO PASS

There have been many prophetic words that have obviously not come to pass and that were inaccurate. In fact, notable Charismatic leaders delivered many of these prophecies in a public forum. They delivered incorrect prophecies, the words were not fulfilled, and, as a result, they brought reproach upon themselves and upon the whole Charismatic Movement.

Here is what we need to consider as we are evaluating the prophetic from a New Testament, not Old Testament, system of testing: even though these leaders delivered inaccurate prophecies this does not confirm that they are operating as false prophets. Under the Old Covenant, prophets were speaking as direct representatives of the voice of God. The Old Testament prophet was one of the key ways the people heard from God. If the prophet was inaccurate or delivered false messages, this was no mistake to be received lightly. The prophet was guilty of misrepresenting God and, as a result, would be punished accordingly.

Again, in the Old Testament context, humankind was dependent upon the prophetic mediator to actually hear from God. Now, because of the shed blood of Christ and His atoning work on Calvary, all of humanity has been granted access to hear from God. Scripture offers the comprehensive revelation of who God is and establishes a standard of His character, nature, and instruction.

In the New Covenant, prophets are not speaking directly on God's behalf; hence, the consequences are not as harsh. It becomes problematic when we use a selective, unrepresentative set of examples of prophecy, focusing solely on the missed or inaccurate prophecies.

While acknowledging the false, we should also celebrate the true and accurate. Major leaders have received prophetic words that have resulted in the planting of 10,000 churches in Mozambique, 10,000 churches in Kenya, thousands of churches in China, thousands of churches in Argentina, and thousands of churches in Brazil. These scores of thousands of churches have resulted in millions of new believers coming to Christ.

We cannot afford to deny one of the most important emphases of Scripture—*the voice of the Lord*—in the hearts of the people, for *"My sheep hear My voice"* (John 10:27 NKJV).

# HEARING GOD'S VOICE TODAY

When I read the works of both cessationists and continuationists, they are both clearly committed to the Bible. Yet, because of their hermeneutics, they end up interpreting the same passages with different understandings. Both perspectives are undoubtedly committed to the all-sufficiency of Scripture, yet their hermeneutics lead them to opposite conclusions regarding the place of miracles, healings, tongues, prophecy, prophets, and apostles.

Let me illustrate my point. Many cessationists believe that the concept of God speaking directly to His people today is a false doctrine that is completely unwarranted by Scripture. Even though the goal seems to be preserving the sufficiency of Scripture—asserting that there is no reason to entertain any forms of "fresh revelation" beyond what has been clearly stated in the written Word—they deny the possibility of God speaking today through any other medium extraneous to the written Scripture.

Again, the context of "God speaking" is *not* providing information that is in addition or contradictory to the canon of Scripture. Continuationist scholar Jon Ruthven writes,

> When we examine Reformation theology, hastily forged as it was, in the heat of polemics and persecution, and measure it against the emphases of Scripture (believed to be the prime source of authority for Protestants), then we can see the essential flaws. Again, the emphasis markers of the Bible are the temptation narratives, the common plot line of narratives, central characteristics of biblical role models (Heb. 11), conceptual repetitions, space devoted, summary statements, goal statements, and the covenants, etc. All of these emphasis markers point to the primal biblical experience: *The New Covenant Spirit that causes us to hear and to know God, resulting in our being empowered to fulfill His word of commission.*[33]

Having read both the cessationist and continuationist arguments, I am convinced the hermeneutic of Ruthven is faithful to the emphasis and clear meaning of the Bible.

## WE CANNOT DISCREDIT THE WHOLE BECAUSE OF THE PART

Typical arguments aimed against the validity of the prophet today—especially in regards to those who occupy the office of a prophet—involve attacking the quality of the witnesses by laying out the weaknesses in the witnesses. In other words, many embrace the idea that because there are false prophets, and because there are men and women who have prophesied falsely, *all* contemporary prophets must, in turn, be false.

We cannot parade the moral failures of some of the Charismatics as representative of the whole movement. This has already been discussed in great detail, as the argument prevents us from examining some of the deeper theological issues at hand. Sadly, the validity of the New Testament prophetic office or prophetic ministry is never adequately addressed. Prophecy is tossed "under the bus," along with the entire Charismatic Movement, assuming that all adherents embrace the prosperity gospel of health and wealth. But this is simply not true. Additionally, we cannot make accurate statements concerning the legitimacy of prophecy today because of erroneous prophetic words. Again, the whole suffers because of the negative "part."

Looking back at some of the early Pentecostal leaders, yes, there were undeniably moral issues that are abhorrent. One could review the words of Charles Parham spoken against William J. Seymour, noting in passing that Parham was a supporter of and sympathizer with the Ku Klux Klan. But again, this would be like using the same logic against Martin Luther for his anti-Semitism. None of these behaviors are acceptable, but they should not be used to discredit an entire movement, in the same way that Luther's character flaws and incorrect positions do not discredit the whole of Reformation thought and theology.

> *The standard of experience is never sufficient to judge an entire movement or a biblical truth. This is lazy theology.*

Likewise, the same false standard that is applied to those involved in healing ministry is applied to those operating in the prophetic ministry of a prophetic office. Healing ministry, by default, tends to be placed under the banner of the Word of Faith Movement, the prosperity gospel, and "health and wealth." This does not take into account the many individuals who have operated in the Holy Spirit's healing power and who did not adhere to any of the aforementioned schools of thought.

Similarly, prophecy as a whole will be unfortunately discredited because of the prophet who had a moral failure, made a false prophecy, or blatantly propagated error, or, even worse, heresy. However, the standard of experience is never sufficient to judge an entire movement or a biblical truth. This is lazy theology, as it does not even demand an earnest investigation of the scriptural text. Rather than making theological arguments, most assaults fired at prophetic ministry are based on false prophecies or the character of those who move in the prophetic. As unfortunate as such examples are, they do not let us off the hook that easily about the modern availability of prophecy.

## AUGUSTINE ON PROPHECY

Augustine, writing in the fifth century, believed prophecy was still a gift the church was experiencing during his time. He considered prophecy to be "a free manifestation of the Holy Spirit by which some people receive a communicable intelligence of truths connected with our salvation but impervious to any natural understanding."[34]

Likewise, prophecy here can take many forms: a revelation, knowledge, foretelling, or teaching, which means that what is spoken of today in the Pentecostal and Charismatic churches finds a parallel in Augustine. A prophecy may bring a revelation of an unknown nature, bringing knowledge of some kind—perhaps the knowledge of what God wanted to do in a specific context, knowledge of direction to take in ministry, knowledge about the future, an insight into teaching, or an insight given during the message. Many healings were connected to prophecy.[35] Augustine has much more in common with continuationism than he does with cessationism.

## How Prophecy Touches Nations and Advances the Gospel Today

Having addressed this subject biblically and theologically, I want to add to the defense from personal experience. I gave two prophetic words, one to Heidi Baker and one to Leif Hetland, which catapulted them into new destinies in the Kingdom of God. Strong manifestations of the Spirit accompanied both words. The power of God was so strong it caused manifestations to come upon them immediately, resulting in giving them faith to do what the prophetic word indicated. As a result, *each* of them has led over one million people to the Lord. This is not a testimony to me, but it simply affirms the validity of the prophetic ministry and the gospel-advancing fruit it produces on a global scale.

Another example from my personal life came the night before I was going to fly to Toronto to speak for the first time. I was very afraid that God would not use me. Before I left for Toronto, a friend of mine, Richard Holcomb, called me and said, "Randy, I have the second most powerful word I have ever had for you. The Lord says, 'Test Me now! Test Me now! Test Me now! Do not be afraid, I will back you up. I want your eyes to be opened to see My resources for you in the heavenlies, even as Elisha prayed for Gehazi's eyes to be opened. And do not become anxious because when you become anxious you can't hear Me.'"

This word so changed me. I met the small team the next morning and told them, "We are going on an apostolic missions trip. We are going to see more than we have ever seen in our lives." The faith to make such a statement was created by the prophetic word.

Again, in 2001, another prophecy significantly influenced my life. I came to believe I was to resign the church my wife and I had started and move again. This would prove to be a shock, a surprise to all of us, except to my daughter who had had a prophetic dream about our relocation before we received the prophetic word to move. Her prophetic dream made it easier for her to accept that the move was God's will.

> *Prophetic words will never contradict or go against what is written in the canon of Scripture; they do not add or subtract, only clarify.*

Through an additional number of prophetic words, dreams, and experiences, my family came to understand that we were to leave our church and move halfway across the nation to start over when I was fifty years old.

Let me propose the following questions about these accounts of prophecy in action:

How would the Bible give Leif Hetland the specific directive to go into areas of darkness where he would be light and where he would be like a bulldozer, making a way for the gospel where there had previously been no way?

How would the Bible be able to give Heidi Baker the faith to believe that God was going to give her the nation of Mozambique, that there would be hundreds of churches and thousands of people coming to Christ?

How could the Bible alone give me the direction to know that I was to move across the country and start a healing ministry?

These kinds of specific directives are dependent upon the present-day gift of prophecy, a gift that the Bible describes as having this kind of function. Remember, prophetic words will *never* contradict or go against what is written in the canon of Scripture; they do not add or subtract, only clarify.

Leif Hetland and Heidi Baker received prophetic words that, though they were not specifically written out in chapter/verse form in Scripture, confirmed a biblical calling on both of their lives and ministries—to preach the gospel of Jesus Christ in global arenas where the masses would receive Christ's salvation.

## Summary

God still speaks to His people today through prophetic ministry and the prophetic office. When we hear about people who have made false prophecies, we should not immediately assume that they are false prophets who are apostate and heretical. In the New Testament, the standards for evaluating prophecies are different from the Old Testament. This should give us grace, not to make excuses for false doctrine or inaccurate prophecies, but to study what Scripture teaches about the New Testament prophetic ministry and use that as our final standard for evaluating whether it is valid today.

## Power Principles

1.  There is a difference between Old Testament and New Testament prophecy. If we do not understand the difference, we will apply a false method of evaluation to judging prophecy today.

2.  Just because someone has delivered a false or inaccurate prophetic word, this does not make him or her a

false prophet. While we should never condone giving false prophecies, we likewise must give grace to those who are endeavoring to learn how to accurately move in the New Testament prophetic gifting.

3. Prophecy will never contradict Scripture; however, it will provide supernatural clarity and confirmation on very specific situations that we are seeking God's guidance on.

*Chapter 5*

# MODERN APOSTLES

*Examining how the apostolic office was not limited
to the twelve men chosen by Christ, and how it was
intended to continue as a gift to the church.*

In his book *On the Cessation of the Charismata*, Jon Ruthven thoroughly addressed and proved that the arguments targeted against modern apostles, and the apostolic, were unbiblical.[36] I believe that Ruthven's work is the gold standard for the continuationist position. It confronts timeless issues that, unfortunately, cessationists have not addressed. Works like Ruthven's do not pretend that every person operating in an "apostolic office" today is legitimate. Their calling is between them and God.

However, as we have discovered thus far, one of the most common ways to discredit an office such as prophet or apostle is to point out examples of people, both past and present, who have claimed these titles and have either embraced heresy, fallen into moral failure, or demonstrated some other type of un-Christlike behavior. To confront these critical issues, *straw man* arguments are insufficient. We must approach them with a solid exegesis of the biblical passages and the resultant arguments.

## B. B. WARFIELD AND COUNTERFEIT MIRACLES

My aim in writing this is to present you with a user-friendly guide to the issues at hand, not some type of comprehensive, academic work. However, there is a level of scholarship that we *all* need to embrace if we are going to walk through some of these controversial topics with scriptural integrity and clarity on how to respond to some of the different arguments.

Dr. Ruthven views other modern cessationists as echoes of noted cessationist B. B. Warfield. He sees Warfield as the zenith of cessationist arguments, and therefore uses Warfield as the basis for his study of cessationism. Ruthven points out that B. B. Warfield's arguments in his noted work *Counterfeit Miracles* were unbiblical, violated Warfield's own hermeneutic, and were based upon two diverging approaches in regards to his historical model—one for biblical history and a different one for post-apostolic history.

Warfield applied the higher-critical method when approaching the post-apostolic history, but he refused to use it for the biblical history. His historical method was both contradictory and inconsistent. Ruthven points out that Warfield only dedicated *six pages* to the biblical texts in *Counterfeit Miracles*. The point here is that one of the most popular and influential works on assaulting the continuation of the power gifts of the Spirit and the apostolic office is a flawed, incomplete work.

In his approach, Ruthven also deals with many biblical texts that refute cessationism that Warfield did not consider. When it comes to evaluating whether or not the apostolic office is valid for today, I would invite modern cessationists to strongly reconsider the targets of their attacks. Instead of making the thrust of our emphasis identifying names and calling out leaders, let us be wholly committed to a *sola Scriptura* approach to the text.

Let us briefly review Ruthven's rebuttal to cessationism, as such is a prime example of honest, biblical scholarship in action. Through his unique approach, he sets out to:

- to re-evaluate the historical evolution of Warfield's cessationism and the concept of miracle on which it depends;

- to examine Warfield's cessationist polemic itself; and then

- to test it for internal consistency with respect to its concept of miracle, its historical method, and its biblical hermeneutics; and

- to scan a few representative passages of Scripture that summarize the recurring theme in the New Testament that spiritual gifts are granted for the advancement of God's Kingdom and the maturity of the church until the end of this present age.[37]

Many refuse to deal with Ruthven's approach to the issue of cessationism, and, as a result, true and necessary dialogue never takes place.

## QUALIFICATIONS OF AN APOSTLE

I have heard cessationists present three conditions or qualifications for one to be an apostle. They are 1) an apostle had to be an eyewitness to the resurrected Christ, 2) an apostle had to be appointed personally by Jesus, and 3) an apostle had to be able to authenticate his apostleship by working miracles. Let us examine each qualification, one at a time.

*Qualification #1: An apostle had to be an eyewitness to the resurrected Christ.* In regards to this qualification, we cannot confuse the requirements for replacing one of the original twelve apostles, Judas, with the qualifications for an apostle who was not one of the twelve. The requirements discussed in the context of replacing Judas are unique to the initial twelve apostles, as they had a unique role in the history of the church. That said, many others who were called apostles in the New Testament had not seen the resurrected Christ.

*Qualification #2: An apostle had to be appointed personally by Jesus.* Regarding the second qualification, true apostles were called by Jesus, and, as such, were anointed by Him, equipping them for their role in the church. When people are called to the ministry, as many denominations believe God calls their pastors and priests, this is another way of saying Jesus has appointed them. Like pastors and priests, apostles are also called or appointed by Jesus today.

*Qualification #3: An apostle had to be able to authenticate his apostleship by working miracles.* Regarding the third qualification, though apostles were anointed to work miracles, they were not the only ones anointed to do so. Evangelists also worked signs and wonders. In addition, in 1 Corinthians 12:28 there are those who are called "workers of miracles" and those with "gifts of healing." These are in the same list as the apostles and reference someone other than the apostles.

## WAS PAUL THE LAST APOSTLE?

Some treat Paul's reference to being the last of the apostles as a reason why there cannot be any more apostles today. This is nothing more than poor reasoning. Paul perceived his authority to be equal to the authority of the twelve, and, as such, he was completing the unique role of this unique group. Yet, Paul calls others "apostles," some of whom received their apostleship through Paul.

The other apostles who are mentioned in the Bible are not functioning in the same capacity as the original twelve and Paul. These include the other seventy (see Luke 10:1), Andronicus (see Rom. 16:7), Apollos (see 1 Cor. 4:6), Barnabas (see Acts 14:1-14), Epaphroditus (see Phil. 2:25-30), James, the Lord's brother (see Gal. 1:19; Acts 12:17; 15:14-34; 21:17-21), Junia, who was a woman (see Rom. 16:7), Silas (see 1 Thess. 1:1; 2:6; 2 Thess. 1:1), and Timothy (see 1 Thess. 1:1; 2:6; 3:2; 1 Cor. 16:10-11).

> *Paul calls others "apostles," some of whom received their apostleship through Paul.*

Many of these are often called *representatives* in the New International Version, but the word is *apostle*, and it is translated as such in the margin of the Revised Version and called *apostles* by Young's Literal Translation of the Holy Bible. Thus, there are eighty-one people called apostles (noun) or apostled (sent out, in the verb form) in the New Testament other than the twelve.

For those who do not embrace the modern apostolic office, they do not consider these people mentioned above as apostles. Rather, they see these individuals as messengers of the churches. However, Scripture sees them as apostles.

## THE APOSTLE'S PURPOSE

*Consequently, you are no longer foreigners and aliens, but fellow citizens with God's people and members of God's household, built on the foundation of the apostles and*

THE ESSENTIAL GUIDE TO THE POWER OF THE HOLY SPIRIT

> *prophets, with Christ Jesus Himself as the chief corner-stone. In Him the whole building is joined together and rises to become a holy temple in the Lord. And in Him you too are being built together to become a dwelling in which God lives by His Spirit.* (Ephesians 2:19-22)

Those who reject the validity of modern apostles would claim that the primary purpose of the apostle was to write Scripture. The cessationist understanding of Ephesians 2:19-22 is that the teaching of the apostles and prophets was included into a body of doctrine, and these stand as the foundation upon which the church is built. Therefore, there can be no more apostles and prophets lest there be more added to the foundation, resulting in an open canon of Scripture—where the text could be added to or subtracted from.

Ruthven rejects this view, providing a strong rationale for the rejection of this Reformation understanding regarding the foundation upon which the church is being built.[38] He points out that the Ephesians 2:19-22 passage by analogy contradicts the cessationists' point of view. The problem is: "1) The 'joining' of *all* elements of the building/temple *in Christ who is the foundation* and 2) the clear references to Christ as being the *last and final* stone in the building/temple."[39]

The problem with the first analogy is that it points to the whole church, and cannot be limited to the first century since the church could not be the whole church if it only included the first-century believers. The problem with the second analogy is that Christ is to be the capstone—the last stone placed in the structure. This would mean the work of Christ was to be ongoing until the *parousia*, His second coming. This upsets the cessationists' understanding of the foundation, requiring that the gifts of the apostles and prophets to continue until the return of Christ.

If the cessationist understanding of the foundation is applied, the result would be the foundation *was already laid*, past tense when Paul was writing. This would mean Paul did not have the authority "to say that apostleship and prophecy no longer existed, for he himself would no longer be an apostle."[40]

Ruthven goes on to point out that only three (Matthew, John, and Peter) of the twelve apostles wrote any Scripture at all, and that they wrote only 16 percent of the words contained in the New Testament. The apostle Paul wrote 43 percent of the words in the New Testament, and he did not satisfy all the criteria in Acts 1 for the replacement for Judas.[41] Non-apostles wrote 41 percent of the New Testament.[42] Paul does not meet the "Acts 1 criteria"; he was not with Jesus during His earthly ministry. I am including him as an apostle, however, and his writings are included in the 59 percent of Scripture written by apostles.[43]

## APOSTOLIC AUTHORITY, THE PROPHETIC VOICE, AND WRITING SCRIPTURE

The foundation, which the apostles and prophets built upon, is misunderstood when their primary purpose is to be writers of Scripture. Consider that there are ten times throughout Scripture where the Holy Spirit used prophecy to inspire the Scriptures, but there are 153 times when the Spirit inspires other types of prophetic utterances that are not connected to becoming Scripture.

The Scripture gives other reasons for prophetic utterances too: to praise and glorify God (see Acts 2:14); for strengthening, encouragement, and comfort (see 1 Cor. 14; Acts 15:32); and for equipping Christians for the work of ministry (see Eph. 4:12-13). Prophecy is also to reveal the secrets of hearts, resulting in effective evangelism (see 1 Cor. 14:24-25). None of the purposes that the New Testament gives for prophecy mentions the writing of the New Testament.[44]

Furthermore, when all the references to prophecy in the book of Acts are considered, not one of the prophecies or their narrator indicates that they were intended as a "foundational doctrine" upon which the church would be built. Ruthven states,

> There is no indication from these texts whatsoever that the *essential function* of prophecy was to serve as oral Scripture until it could be reduced to writing. If, indeed, the function of the gifts determine their duration, then it is clear that demanding the cessation of apostles and prophets because of their input into the process of writing Scripture is based on the most tenuous NT indications. The strong and explicit functions of these gifts seem to evidence, rather, their continuation until their tasks are complete at the *Parousia*. Ephesians continues its description of apostles and prophets in 4:11-13 where it describes the gifts being given to the Church *until (mechri) we all* enter the eschatological state of "attaining to the *whole measure* of the *fullness* of Christ."[45]

Therefore, the foundation that the church is built upon is not the body of doctrine written by the apostles and prophets. If the apostles and the prophets themselves are not what is meant by the foundation upon which the church is built, then what is it built upon? Ruthven further explains,

> Nevertheless, the Bible in general, and Ephesians in particular, does not identify *itself* as the foundational core of the Church. Rather, the *disclosure experience of Christ,* although within its biblical framework, is truly the

foundation of the Church. St. Paul was concerned that Christians' faith rested *not* on *words,* but on "a demonstration of the Spirit's power" (1 Cor. 2:14). This strongly suggests that normatively, a system of propositions, however true they may be, is not the basis for faith; rather it is *Christ Himself,* through the *activity* of the *Spirit* of Christ, with a strong overtone of revelation that characterizes this foundation.[46]

## DEALING WITH THE REAL ARGUMENTS

Cessationists should respond to the arguments of Ruthven in *On the Cessation of the Charismata: The Protestant Polemic on Post-Biblical Miracles.* The arguments of Wayne Grudem should also be answered in "Should Christians Expect Miracles Today? Objection and Answers from the Bible" in *The Kingdom and the Power: Are Healing and the Spiritual Gifts Used By Jesus and the Early Church Meant for the Church Today?*[47]

Time does not allow me to lay out all these powerful arguments for the continuationist position regarding the gifts of the Spirit and the apostolic office. I encourage you to study the arguments that lay the biblical basis for the continuation of all the gifts of the Spirit.

## EXAMPLES OF MODERN APOSTLES

If we do not use the Reformation's understanding of the title "apostle," but instead use the New Testament as our standard definition, then there is no reason to deny the office for today's church and for the church's history.

For example, though St. Patrick of Ireland did not use the title of apostle, he had that function. John Wesley would qualify as well, while George Whitefield would be better titled as an evangelist.

Hudson Taylor's work in China appears apostolic, as does Rolland and Heidi Baker's work in Mozambique. Dennis Balcomb's role in China looks apostolic, and Sophal Ung and Ted Olbrich, both in Cambodia, have ministries that appear to be apostolic in nature.

When I met Pastor Enoch Adeboye in Lagos, Nigeria, it was difficult to comprehend what God had done through him. He took over a church of about five hundred people and grew it to millions. This movement spans both countries and nations. The church building is 1.2 miles by 1.8 miles, with seating for four million people. Presently they are building a facility twice this size under one roof that will seat eight million. Their monthly prayer meeting draws over a million people every first Friday of the month. Miracles and healings are very important to the growth and emphasis of this flourishing church. The title *pastor* seems inadequate for Pastor Adeboye. He is called the General Overseer. Not all denominational overseers are apostolic in function, but Pastor Adeboye appears to have an apostolic function.

> *Writing Scripture was not one of the main items on the job description for apostles.*

Some of the missionaries, both past and present, were apostolic too, even though their theological frameworks would prohibit them from using such a title. What we have often done is create non-biblical terms to replace the proper biblical definitions for the same job description.

Ultimately, when it comes to determining the legitimacy for the apostolic office today, it is important to consider that writing Scripture was not one of the main items on the job description for apostles. This was only for a select few of the apostles, not even the complete group of the original twelve.

## Summary

In order to embrace the modern apostolic office, it is important for us to carefully evaluate the different functions of the apostles in the New Testament. Some wrote Scripture, while others did not. There are twelve that remain key cornerstones in the establishment of the church that Jesus built. Yet, while there were twelve apostles of Christ—and these twelve remain exceptional above the rest—Scripture also reveals that there were other apostles who, though not instrumental in establishing the original church infrastructure, were still key leaders in building the church and preaching the gospel.

## Power Principles

1. Scripture lists several examples of apostles who were not part of the original twelve, demonstrating that the apostolic office was not confined to the twelve men who were with Jesus during His earthly ministry.

2. Ephesians 2:19-22 needs to be understood in its correct context if we are going to embrace the office of apostles in the church today. The key is identifying the true foundation and cornerstone upon which the faith was established.

3. Many missionaries, church planters, and pastors today function in an apostolic office, but may not assign their role this unique designation or definition due to their theologies.

*Chapter 6*

# IS SPEAKING IN TONGUES FOR TODAY?

*Demystifying one of the most controversial gifts of the Holy Spirit and recognizing the power it releases in a believer's everyday life.*

Because the gift of tongues is quite possibly the most controversial demonstration of the Holy Spirit's power, I want to give sufficient space for us to review the different aspects of this supernatural phenomenon.

## HEAVENLY TONGUES OR KNOWN LANGUAGES?

When speaking in tongues is discussed, many consider it to mean only one thing: the ability to supernaturally speak a human language, a language not learned by a natural means. The problem is that this limited definition does not distinguish between *xenolalia*, which is speaking in a known language, and *glossolalia*, which is speaking in an unknown language.

It is true that early Pentecostals believed the Lord was giving them foreign languages to speak that would enable them to evangelize the nations. It is also true they were disappointed. It turned out that their tongues were not the languages of men. At that time (after the disappointment), tongues were believed to be the languages of heaven or of angels (see 1 Cor. 13:1). It is true that the early Pentecostals changed their understanding of tongues. It is also true that some people have supernaturally received *xenolalia*, tongues of known languages.

For example, Surpresa Sithole, Heidi and Rolland Baker's main associate—who is both very apostolic and very prophetic—speaks fourteen languages. He only learned two of those languages in a natural way. He received all of the other languages through the supernatural empowerment of the Holy Spirit—he could both speak in a different language *and* understand what he was saying. The language, once received, remained a language that he could continue to speak and understand.

Though this is undeniably a sign, and it is supernatural, it does not appear to be the kind of tongues Paul is specifically addressing in 1 Corinthians 12–14. In this context, the speaker does not understand the tongues being spoken or prayed. According to Paul, one must actually pray for the understanding of what is being spoken.

The tongues of 1 Corinthians are not like the tongues of Acts 2, where there was no need for someone to interpret, for all of the people present heard the apostles speaking in their own languages. The gift of interpretation is not a natural means, but is itself a supernatural gift. The interpreter is not interpreting a language that he or she already understood. When someone is interpreting an understood, known language, there is nothing supernatural in the interpretation, and there is no reason to call it a gift. Instead, it would be a natural or learned ability.

For this reason, reducing the gift to a human ability rather than a grace, many Pentecostals and Charismatics would agree that *glossolalia* (speaking in an unknown tongue) is not an actual human language. Thus it cannot be evaluated, interpreted, or translated like any form of existing language. Many Pentecostals and Charismatics would agree that speaking in tongues is actually the language of angels. However, they would not rule out the gift of *xenolalia*.

> *Many Pentecostals and Charismatics would agree that speaking in tongues is actually the language of angels.*

## Xenolalia: Supernaturally Speaking and Understanding Known Languages

Just in my limited circle of relationships, I have heard of three people who received *xenolalia*, and it remained an ability they had from the moment they received the gift. One of them was Surpresa Sithole, as mentioned earlier.

Another was a missionary from Paducah, Kentucky, who was in Latin America. A prophecy told him to pick up the bulletin, which was written in Spanish, and read it. He knew that he did not have the ability to do so. Immediately when he tried, however, he received the ability to speak and understand Spanish.

A third person, who I know personally, used to work for me and was the son of a missionary to the native peoples of Brazil. When he heard some young people from Youth with a Mission speaking in English, which he could not understand at the time, he asked God for the language. Overnight he received the ability to speak and understand English.

I have heard of others who had similar experiences as those. They were not only able to speak the new language one time or during an isolated instance, but after the original gifting happened, it continued as a lasting gift in their lives.

## A FRINGE AND HERETICAL MOVEMENT?

Some will mention the unknown tongues and expressions of *glossolalia* spoken by schizophrenics, voodoo doctors of Africa, Buddhist monks, and Mormons. In turn, they denounce tongues in any context as ecstatic speech that is often characteristic of fringe, heretical groups. In turn, cessationists have announced that orthodox, historical Christianity, by and large, has not embraced speaking in tongues.

> *Tongues became one of the common denominator experiences that believers in different mainline denominations shared.*

This is patently not true. The mainline denominations after the Charismatic Movement occurred did not consider the practices of the gifts of the Spirit as heretical—particularly speaking in tongues. In fact, speaking in tongues became one of the common denominator experiences that believers in different mainline denominations shared.

Instead of excommunicating members who moved in the gifts, they created Charismatic renewal movements for the pastors and laity in their respective denominations to accommodate them. These were created among the American Baptist, United Methodist, Presbyterian and Reformed denominations, Roman Catholic, as well as many others.

It simply is not true to say irrational and ecstatic speech has been associated *only* with fringe or heretical groups. Whereas the

Pentecostal Movement began among Protestants, primarily among the poor and the less educated, such *glossolalic* speech began among Roman Catholics in their universities, among the academic community, and even among their most highly-educated Cardinals.[48]

## ST. AUGUSTINE'S THEOLOGY OF TONGUES AND THE SUPERNATURAL

Once again, tongues as expressed in Acts 2 is not the exclusive manifestation of this phenomenon in Scripture. First Corinthians 12–14 introduces readers to the *unknown tongues* of a private prayer language, as well as an unknown tongue accompanied by a supernatural interpretation.

Cessationist leaders have tried to build a case against speaking in tongues, using statements by Augustine such as, "That was the sign (tongues) that was given, and it passed." Again, this is in reference to the expression of tongues in Acts 2. Such a statement should be seen in light of Augustine's Retractions in his last book, *The City of God,* where he acknowledges that the gifts of healing, miracles, and other gifts had not passed away as he had written when he was much younger.[49] Augustine's experience had proved his earlier statements were wrong. In fact, history tells us that Augustine experienced a healing and deliverance ministry in his later years.[50]

One cannot build a solid case against the gifts of the Spirit using Augustine, because Augustine was more a continuationist than he was a cessationist.[51]

### Augustine's Theology of the Baptism of the Spirit

Joseph Bentivegna, in his amazing study on Augustine, notes that Augustine believed the baptism of the Holy Spirit was available for all Christians and characterized the new times of the church.[52]

It was only available to those who were already baptized; hence, it was subsequent to conversion.[53]

The purpose of the baptism of the Spirit was to empower Christians to enable them to live a holy lifestyle, including the power of God to work healings and miracles.[54] He described it as "an extraordinary and irresistible intervention of the supreme might of the Holy Spirit that enables us to profess and practice in a plenary and practical manner the divine lordship of Jesus Christ."[55]

Augustine further believed several doctrinal points were

> *Augustine believed the baptism of the Holy Spirit was available for all Christians and characterized the new times of the church.*

important regarding the baptism of the Holy Spirit.[56] Again, these points reinforce the fact that Augustine was a continuationist. In his Retractions, he confirmed this in many ways as already noted. One of his most plain statements was, "Nobody is entitled to say that our Lord Jesus Christ does not perform such marvels even nowadays...even now the Spirit is at work in the whole variety of His free manifestations."[57]

### Augustine on Speaking in Tongues

When it came to speaking in tongues, Augustine did not believe that the gift of tongues—the ability to speak all known languages—was still happening in his day.[58] He did believe that tongues still occurred, however, but not like in the book of Acts.

Augustine acknowledged that the expression of tongues similar to 1 Corinthians 12–14 was possible and would be equivalent to prophecy when there was an interpretation given. The interpretation was what made the tongue intelligible and was not based upon the person understanding a language through natural ability, but through an interpretative grace of the Spirit.

He believed that the difference in the administration of the gifts "depended upon the times, persons, and places of worship."[59] Augustine did not believe all of the gifts of the Spirit were limited to those recorded in Scripture, for he says, "By His ascension into heaven Jesus Christ has opened, as it were, the cataracts of His gifts, whose inventory cannot possibly be made."[60]

## Augustine's Supernatural Experiences

The following expressions of the Spirit's power were particularly important to Augustine because he had personal experiences with each of them—dreams and visions, miracles, casting out devils, ecstasy and resting in the Spirit, prophecy, and discernment of spirits.[61]

He describes dreams and visions as "cases in which our soul is assumed by the Spirit, who presents to us in a divine manner the things that He wants to be seen by us."[62] That these were common experiences in his life was indicated by his statement, "They are so many... that I have not enough time to report all the cases of this experience."[63]

## Augustine on Miracles

Augustine's definition of miracles was as follows: "I call miracle whatever proves to be arduous and uncommon and above the expectation (*spem*) and capacity of those who admire it."[64] He noted something that is as true today as it was in his day: "People who do not experience them (miracles) directly find it difficult to accept them, although such miracles are reported by some Christians to other fellow believers."[65]

### Reading of Miracles

Around AD 424, Augustine introduced the reading of miracles to his diocese and into neighboring communities' churches;[66] many churches in past revivals and renewal movements did this. He had many pastors tell him they would read to their churches his published accounts of the healings and miracles in his services. Augustine's intention and understanding was that these readings were "to give due glory and honour to the Lord."[67]

In summary, though Augustine early in his career made some statements that seemed to be cessationist in nature, he reversed his opinion and became a continuationist, not just in theory, but also in practice.

## CHANGING PERSPECTIVES ON THE SUPERNATURAL

Like Augustine, Southern Baptist scholar Robert Culpepper reversed his earlier opinion regarding the charismata. He wrote:

A second reason for rejecting the theory of the temporary nature of the gifts is that there is good evidence for believing that the Holy Spirit still bestows His gifts upon His people when there is an attitude of openness and expectancy. I once viewed the miraculous manifestations of the Spirit as temporary in design and expressed this view in an article on "The Problem of Miracles" in the April 1956 issue of the Review and Expositor [this is the scholarly publication of The Southern Baptist

> There is good evidence for believing that the Holy Spirit still bestows His gifts upon His people when there is an attitude of openness and expectancy.
> —ROBERT CULPEPPER

Theological Seminary, Louisville, KY]. However, what I
have seen, heard, read, thought, felt and experienced since
then has convinced me that I was wrong. When fact and
theory collide, the better part of wisdom is to revise or
discard the theory in the light of the facts rather than
stubbornly to hold to the theory in defiance of the facts.
In my judgment, views of the temporary nature of the
gifts should be buried.[68]

## THE LANGUAGE OF TONGUES

Biblically speaking, the tongues of 1 Corinthians 12 and 14
do appear to be irrational, but the tongues of Pentecost were not.
Tongues are not always ecstatic.

In my dialogue with Pentecostals and Charismatics around
the world, I have found that for those who experienced tongues
at the time they were baptized in the Holy Spirit, the tongues
seemed more ecstatic. However, for those who received the prayer
language of tongues, but not at the time of their baptism in the
Holy Spirit, their experience did not seem to be emotional or
ecstatic. This was my case when I received my prayer language
at age nineteen. However, I did not receive the baptism with the
Holy Spirit until I was thirty-two, again at thirty-nine, and again
at forty-one.

## TONGUES: A SIGN OF APOSTLESHIP?

Some see tongues as a sign that authenticates the apostles
as messengers of the true gospel in Mark 16:20. The problem
with this reasoning is that it is not the apostles who are being
validated—rather it is the gospel of the Kingdom itself that is
being authenticated.

Cessationists might argue that the gift of tongues made another provision for God to unveil His truth to the church prior to the canonization of the New Testament. However, this understanding of tongues is not congruent with the 1 Corinthians 12 and 14 perspective of an unknown heavenly language, but rather a miracle

> To reduce tongues to a sign authenticating apostleship, or confirming the legitimacy of theological doctrine, is a misunderstanding of the actual scriptural expression of tongues.

that causes individuals unlearned in a language to be able to supernaturally speak it. This is a half-truth, as there was a supernatural demonstration of a linguistic miracle that took place on the day of Pentecost.

Paul, in 1 Corinthians 14:2, states that tongues are not directed to people but to God: *"For anyone who speaks in a tongue does not speak to men but to God."* Therefore, the message would not be doctrinal in nature, but would rather be an expression of adoration, worship, and praise. To reduce tongues to a sign authenticating apostleship, or confirming the legitimacy of theological doctrine, is a misunderstanding of the actual scriptural expression of tongues.

## IS TONGUES THE INITIAL EVIDENCE OF THE BAPTISM IN THE SPIRIT?

When relating tongues to the baptism in the Holy Spirit, not all Pentecostal or Charismatic believers hold to the same theological perspective. It is commonly assumed that everyone who believes in speaking in tongues embraces the position that speaking in tongues is the initial evidence of receiving the baptism of Holy Spirit, and that it has to be subsequent to conversion. This is simply not true. Many Third Wave Evangelicals believe that one can be baptized in the Holy Spirit and not speak in tongues, or that one could speak in tongues and not necessarily be baptized in the Holy Spirit.

The cessationist position states that there is one baptism in the Holy Spirit, and this always takes place at conversion. Cessationists use 1 Corinthians 12:13 as the common proof text for this perspective: "For we were all baptized by one Spirit so as to form one body—whether Jews or Gentiles, slave or free—and we were all given the one Spirit to drink."

The problem with this text is that the New Testament speaks of more than one baptism. Hebrews 6:1-2 gives the six apostolic elementary teachings: "Therefore let us leave the elementary teachings about Christ and go on to maturity, not laying again the foundation of repentance from acts that lead to death, and of faith in God, instruction about baptisms, the laying on of hands, the resurrection of the dead, and eternal judgment."

Verse 2 speaks of the doctrine about baptisms (the word baptism is a plural). There were three baptisms spoken of in the New Testament, the baptism into Christ by the Spirit at regeneration, the baptism with water, and the baptism in the Holy Spirit by Jesus. The baptism in 1 Corinthians 12:13 is the baptism into Christ; this is conversion or regeneration. It is a work of the Spirit resulting in the new birth.

## A THEOLOGY OF SPIRIT BAPTISM

Luke is truly the theologian of the Holy Spirit and grants us even greater insight into the different expressions of baptism. His two-volume work is not merely gospel and history; it is theological history written under the unction of the Holy Spirit, and it is as much authoritative as the epistles, which were written to answer local church problems.[69] In properly interpreting and understanding the New Testament, Pentecostals and Charismatics have an advantage because they have an analogous experience to that which the New Testament depicts.

Theologian Clark Pinnock points to this advantage and the legitimacy of its addition to the understanding of Scripture when he writes: "We cannot consider Pentecostalism to be a kind of aberration born of experimental excesses but a 20th century revival of New Testament theology and religion. It has not only restored joy and power to the church but a clearer reading to the Bible as well."[70]

> *We cannot consider Pentecostalism to be a kind of aberration born of experimental excesses but a 20th century revival of New Testament theology and religion. It has not only restored joy and power to the church but a clearer reading to the Bible as well.*
> —CLARK PINNOCK

Luke's theology of the sovereign Spirit does not reveal a consistent pattern of Spirit baptism, either as taught by Pentecostals or by evangelicals. Instead, Luke reveals a diversity of experiences with different patterns. He definitely does not reinforce the classic cessationist argument that the baptism with the Holy Spirit occurs at conversion. Only one of his six accounts of the filling of the Spirit occur at the moment of conversion, that being the account of Cornelius in Acts 10.

Rather, Luke depicts the filling of the Holy Spirit at conversion as an exception, and not the normative way people are filled with the Spirit. In Acts, Luke describes the baptism of the Holy Spirit as a post-conversion experience. This is what is seen at Pentecost in Acts 2, the experience of the persecuted church in Acts 4:29-31, the Spirit coming upon the new believers in Samaria in Acts 8, the Spirit filling Saul in Acts 9, and the filling of the disciples in Acts 19.

It should be noted that Augustine saw the baptism with the Holy Spirit also as a post-conversion event. He wrote, "The outpouring of the pentecostal Spirit in the Church 'remains always an act of mercy and grace.' It is an act of mercy because it presupposes that those upon whom it flows 'have already received the forgiveness of their sins. It is an act of grace because it has no relationship with the assessment of man's merits.'"[71]

John Wesley also saw the baptism with the Holy Spirit as a post-conversion experience. He insisted that one was born of the Spirit at the moment of justification. However, he did not see the Spirit coming into the person as the same experience as the Spirit coming *upon* the person. Wesley's language of baptism in the Spirit developed during the last twenty years of his life. He believed this was the position of the early church fathers and was consistent to the Easter–Pentecost paradigms, with Easter representing forgiveness and regeneration, and Pentecost representing the experience of being filled or baptized with the Holy Spirit.[72]

## Should We Expect or Desire to Speak in Tongues?

Paul admonished, *"Pursue love, and earnestly desire the spiritual gifts"* (1 Cor. 14:1 ESV). Cessationists are leery about this verse in which Paul expresses that he would like *all* believers in Corinth to *earnestly desire* spiritual gifts—which includes speaking in tongues.

Those attempting to devalue the gift of tongues and Paul's positive view of the gift of tongues would go against almost all the translators of the New Testament. Of the twenty-seven translations I consulted, not one translated this verse as an indicative instead of the imperative. They all had it in the imperative command form.

I would rather trust the ability of the hundreds of translators who are Greek specialists than the ability of assorted pastors and self-proclaimed theologians to translate this passage correctly, especially in light of the fact that their presuppositions and biases against tongues rule their translations rather than the actual context of the text.

Paul exhorts the Corinthians to *earnestly desire* the gifts of the Spirit (see 1 Cor. 14:1) and even expresses, "*I wish you all spoke with tongues*" (1 Cor. 14:5 NKJV), affirming that the ability to speak in tongues, as a private prayer language, is available to all. However, there is a difference between the ability to pray in a prayer language for personal edification and connection with God, and the ability to deliver a prophetic message in tongues during a service or gathering. The prophetic expression of tongues is given sovereignly, just as the gift of interpretation of tongues would be.

> *There is a difference between the ability to pray in a prayer language for personal edification and connection with God, and the ability to deliver a prophetic message in tongues during a service or gathering.*

## THE GIFTS OF THE SPIRIT AND GOD'S SOVEREIGNTY

We cannot see the *earnest* pursuit of tongues, or any other gift of the Spirit for that matter, as contradictory to the sovereignty of God. Though Scripture confirms that the Holy Spirit allocates gifts *as He wills* (see 1 Cor. 12:11), this does not mean that we simply yield to His sovereign choice without any expectation on our end. As John Wimber taught, the key to understanding the larger passage in 1 Corinthians 11–14 is to see it in light of the church gathered.[73] There is a difference between *constituted* and *situational* giftings.

The sovereignly given gift context is in relation to whom the Lord chooses in that particular service to manifest an expression of a particular gift. Because the gifts are expressions of the grace of God for the benefit of the people, it is important for the believers to *desire* to be used in these sovereign gifts. The gifts are means for the immanence of God to manifest to His people. They are expressions of the love and power of God helping people in the midst of their problems.

These gifts are not permanent endowments or permanent abilities that the person can utilize at his or her own will. They are often situational. This means that though a gift may manifest in a particular gathering of the local church, that does not mean that person can use that gift at their will. The manifestation of a gift is under the sovereignty of God. It simply is incorrect to see individual members of the body limited to one exclusive gift. This view does not make sense in light of Paul's admonishments to desire spiritual gifts, including tongues and prophecy.

> *The gifts are means for the immanence of God to manifest to His people.*

People who have become Christians have the Holy Spirit; otherwise, they are not Christians. Paul points out this truth in Romans 8:9: *"And if anyone does not have the Spirit of Christ, he does not belong to Christ."* The Holy Spirit in us is the source of every gift, resulting in the possibility of any gift manifesting in the life of a believer. Therefore, we should desire spiritual gifts, and especially the gift of prophecy, because it is so important to edifying the church body.

# MODERN TESTIMONIES OF SPEAKING IN TONGUES

I want to conclude this section with some personal stories about the gift of tongues, which I heard during my ministry travels in 2012.

### An Encounter in Russia

The first was from a woman in Russia, who is the wife of a major apostolic leader who oversees a large network of churches. She was raised in the home of a secular Jewish father, who was both a scientist and an atheist. She became curious about Christians. So she went to the forest where the Christians were meeting during the Soviet Era when the meetings of the unregistered churches were illegal.

In the forest she heard a woman speaking in tongues. In her presence, the young woman felt a presence of peace. She asked the woman what she was doing, and the woman replied, "Praying in tongues." The young woman replied, "I want to do that." The response she got was, "Oh, you can't. You're not holy enough."

However, God had another viewpoint. He sovereignly chose to simultaneously save her and fill her with the Holy Spirit. She began to speak in tongues even though she did not yet understand the gospel and had not yet repented. She had been touched by the presence of God in the worship of the unregistered church.

### The Gift of Tongues Leads to Salvation in Ukraine

Shortly after hearing this story, I traveled to Ukraine where I met a pastor who had planted the largest evangelical (Pentecostal) church in his city, consisting of over several thousand people. Many years before, he had become curious about Christians. So he went to a street where the unregistered church met during the Soviet Era. People were singing in the street. He stepped into their midst to observe. There was no preaching happening, only worship, when all of a sudden he began to simultaneously feel power, joy, and peace as he began to speak in another tongue.

When someone noticed he was not among the known Christians, they took him to their leader. The leader asked, "How long have you been a Christian?" The man replied, "I'm not." The leader asked him how long he had been speaking in tongues, to which he responded, "About five minutes." The leader realized God was doing something sovereign in this man, even though this was not the normal way God worked, not the normal *order solutis*. He still recognized that God, in His sovereignty, had come upon this man.

The leader then explained the gospel to this man, led him in a prayer of confession and repentance, and followed it with explanation. He said, "Do you know what this means? It means that the God who created the universe has come into you and is living with you."

The man became excited about the good news that God had come into him. He went home and gathered together his family, friends, and neighbors. He then spoke in tongues in front of them and told them his story. He said, "The God who created the universe now lives in me, He has forgiven me, and He wants to live in you." He led them to the Lord, and thus began his church, which grew to become the largest church in the city.

## My First Experience with Tongues

My own story regarding tongues is not normative either. I was interested in what God was doing in 1971 through the Jesus Movement, and I had met someone who told me about the gift of tongues in college. I was praying one day at the Baptist church, of which I was the assistant pastor, when I was twenty years old. While I was by myself praying, I uttered a few syllables that I had not intended on saying. It probably did not last more than fifteen to twenty seconds. I had never heard anyone speak in tongues up to that point and wondered if what I had done was actually speak in tongues. It was confusing because I did not experience any power, joy, peace, or ecstasy in any major way.

I opened my Bible to read, and it opened to 1 Corinthians 8:9 where Paul said, *"Be careful, however, that the exercise of your freedom does not become a stumbling block to the weak."* I knew this did not mean I was better or more mature than the others, but that when it came to the gift of tongues, the congregation could be caused to stumble if I told them what had happened to me. However, I was excited about this new gift. I began to spend more time praying in tongues, and soon had told almost all the other young preachers from my association of Baptist churches about what I had experienced. I led most of them into this gift of the Holy Spirit by asking God in prayer.

### Tongues and My Son's Asthma

I had two other experiences that gave me a much greater appreciation for the gift of tongues. The first happened when my oldest child, Joshua, was about three or four years old. He had severe asthma and would wake up at three o'clock every morning in a bad asthma attack, barely able to breath. This happened for about ten years.

We would always pray for him to get him through the asthma attack. One day I was away from home when Josh went into an asthma attack. My wife, DeAnne, began to pray for him. After a bit of time he looked up at her and said, "Mommy, pray the other way!" She responded, "What do you mean?" He said, "You know, Mommy, when you use the words that I don't know what they mean." She responded, "Why?" To which he replied, "Because it works better."

Josh had no theological agenda, no interpretative hermeneutic, no prejudice one way or the other. He just knew that praying in tongues helped alleviate his asthma attacks better than praying in English.

### The Gift of Tongues Gives New Language to Praise

My final story about the gift of tongues goes back to my pastorate at a Baptist church in southern Illinois. I had kept the fact that I prayed in tongues a secret so that I would not be fired. My best friend in the church was a deacon whose mother was not a Pentecostal and neither did she pray in tongues, but she had a Pentecostal theology and believed that one had to have the gift of tongues to be filled or baptized in the Holy Spirit.

Two of her sons were deacons in the church I pastored. She had preached this doctrine to her sons to the point that one of her sons, Tom, was very negative about this gift. One night he was sharing with me his negativity about the subject when I opened up and asked him a series of questions. I said, "Tom, have you ever wanted to praise God more but ran out of titles? Perhaps you had said, 'You are the Alpha and Omega, the Bright and Morning Star, the Lily of the Valley, the Good Shepherd, Emmanuel, Father, Counselor, Almighty God, Everlasting Savior,' but your spirit wanted to continue in praise and your brain couldn't think of anything else to say?" He responded, "Yes."

> **Tongues is a gift, not an attainment.**

I continued, "Tom, tongues are helpful in this situation." Then I said, "Tom, I pray in tongues. I have kept it a secret, but I felt that the fact that your mother is pushing tongues on you as if you're a second-class citizen has made you so closed to the subject that I wanted to suggest another way of thinking about it. Tongues is a gift, not an attainment. It is a crutch we can lean on in our weakness rather than a badge of superiority to be worn proudly. It does not make us more saved, or more sanctified. It is a grace."

I will never forget what happened next. Tom looked at me and said, "Randy, all my adult life I have been against tongues. But after listening to you, for the first time in my life, I can see that this gift could be helpful to me, and I desire to enter into it."

## SIMPLY ASK

The gift of tongues should not be forced upon anyone, nor should it be treated as a pathway to spiritual superiority. It is a gift, plain and simple. God, in His grace, has made it possible for you to pray in a language that is unknown to you, but completely known in heaven.

> *God, in His grace, has made it possible for you to pray in a language that is unknown to you, but completely known in heaven.*

I want to encourage you to simply come before the Lord and ask Him for this wonderful gift. Remember, your God is a good Father. You need not worry about opening yourself up to something evil, demonic, or unbiblical. Take a moment to consider the words of Jesus concerning the Holy Spirit:

*Which of you fathers, if your son asks for a fish, will give him a snake instead? Or if he asks for an egg, will give him a scorpion? If you then, though you are evil, know how to give good gifts to your children, how much more will your Father in heaven give the Holy Spirit to those who ask Him!* (Luke 11:11-13)

Is there some spiritual secret to experiencing the Holy Spirit and receiving this gift? Yes. It is to *simply ask Him for it.* Some people have hands laid on them and begin praying in tongues as they receive impartation. While this approach is certainly biblical, it is not the only way a person can begin walking in this gift. Some have been simply sitting in their bedroom and, in quiet desperation, received this supernatural language.

Remember, the Holy Spirit moves differently upon different people—the one common denominator is to simply *eagerly desire* the gifts of the Spirit (see 1 Cor. 14:1). He always fills and satisfies the hungry!

## Summary

The ability to speak in tongues does not signify spiritual superiority, nor is it necessarily an ecstatic experience that happens to us, over which we have absolutely no control. Misunderstandings about speaking or praying in tongues have kept us from understanding its purpose and activating power in our everyday lives. When we have an incorrect definition of tongues, we will react with confusion, not clarity. Confusion on this particular subject has kept many believers from unwrapping a wonderful gift of grace that supernaturally enriches their prayer lives.

## Power Principles

1. There are different expressions of speaking in tongues, as revealed in Acts 2 and 1 Corinthians 12 and 14.

2. Even though speaking in tongues can take place where someone supernaturally speaks and/or understands a human language that they otherwise would not know, it most commonly refers to a heavenly language that is unknown in the earth, described as "tongues of angels."

3. The baptism of the Holy Spirit is not a one-size-fits-all experience. The Spirit is sovereign, and the experiences He brings are quite diverse. Rather than placing limitations on how He wants to work in our lives, we should eagerly desire for Him to fill us and empower us with His gifts—including the grace of praying in tongues.

*Chapter 7*

# DOES GOD STILL HEAL THE SICK?

*Unlocking a full expression of the gospel's
power through the Holy Spirit's ability to
supernaturally heal disease and sickness.*

We cannot simply reject divine healing because we live in fear of giving people false hope. My question is, Why is it necessary to destroy hope altogether out of fear of *false* hope? Would it not be better to live and die *in hope*, rather than in despair, depression, and hopelessness? The subject of supernatural healing is not simply a matter of people experiencing wholeness or being cured of malady, but it is a question of whether or not we are witnessing the full demonstration of the gospel of the Kingdom as Jesus intended.

## DOES JESUS REBUKE SIGNS AND WONDERS?

We cannot mistake Matthew 16:4 as Jesus rebuking people for desiring signs, wonders, and miracles. In this context, it is true that Jesus rebukes the Pharisees, stating that *"a wicked and adulterous generation looks for a miraculous sign."* The key, however, is to study this verse in its context and understand the nature of the *sign* Jesus was referring to.

As pointed out by New Testament scholar Dr. Craig Keener, this passage is not condemning those who ask for signs to strengthen their faith, but rather those who are seeking reasons to continue in disbelief.[74] The signs referred to in Matthew 16:4 are signs in the natural realm (i.e., weather), not the signs that Jesus was producing.

> *The subject of supernatural healing is not simply a matter of people experiencing wholeness or being cured of malady, but it is a question of whether or not we are witnessing the full demonstration of the gospel of the Kingdom as Jesus intended.*

The belief of the time was that just before God's Kingdom would come, there would be a generation of unbelief. This belief is represented in the language Jesus uses: *"wicked and adulterous generation."* Jesus had just done the signs of a prophet in multiplying food in Matthew 15:29-39.[75] This rebuke is not about Jesus condemning Charismatics and Pentecostals, but, rather, it is an indictment of those who profess to believe but are blatantly denying the things Jesus is doing today.

## THE IMPORTANCE OF FAITH IN JESUS'S HEALINGS

Contrary to the opinion of some, healings in the New Testament often depended upon the recipient's faith—even those accomplished by Jesus Himself. It is true that there are occasions where the faith of the person experiencing the miracle was not involved, but it is also true that the New Testament contains many examples where the faith of the recipient was involved and acknowledged.

In the next few pages, I want to take you through several of Jesus's miracles in order to identify how faith played a vital role in the afflicted individual experiencing God's healing.

**The Roman Centurion's servant.** The centurion's servant was healed in a way that involved his faith. In Matthew 8:13, it states, *"Then Jesus said to the centurion, 'Go! It will be done just as you believed it would.' And his servant was healed at that very hour."*

> *Healings in the New Testament often depended upon the recipient's faith—even those accomplished by Jesus Himself.*

**Woman with the issue of blood.** The woman with the issue of blood was healed by her faith. Matthew 9:22 reads, *"Jesus turned and saw her. 'Take heart, daughter,' He said, 'your faith has healed you.' And the woman was healed from that moment."*

**Two blind men.** The two blind men were also healed in a manner that involved their faith. Matthew 9:29-30 states, *"Then He touched their eyes and said, 'According to your faith will it be done to you'; and their sight was restored."*

**The ten lepers.** We cannot take an example, such as the ten lepers in Luke 17:11-19, and mistakenly assume that only one "expressed faith," yet all were still healed. This is not what the Scripture says. Nowhere does it state that only one expressed faith; rather, it expresses that one returned to express thanks.

The fact that Jesus said to the formerly leprous Samaritan that his faith has made him well in no way indicates that he was the only one of the ten who had faith (see Luke 17:17-19). The fact that faith was instrumental to this one's healing would be paradigmatic to believe it was likewise faith on the part of the other nine that was instrumental to their healing.

**Man at the pool of Bethesda.** The man at the pool at Bethesda is commonly used as an example of not having faith, but there is reason to believe that the man actually did have faith. The reason to believe this is that John's Gospel features only seven signs.[76] All the other signs were preceded by an act of obedience that demonstrated that the people believed in Jesus, and they were, in fact, points of contact for the releasing of faith.

With the other six signs being plainly connected to acts of obedience, they become the paradigm for inferring that when Jesus said to him in John 5:8, *"Get up! Pick up your mat and walk,"* he was healed when he tried to get up. Jesus told him to do three things, then the next verse says he "picked up his mat and walked." The implication is that the healing came when he tried to get up.

The fact that he did not know Jesus's identity does not mean he did not exercise faith in Jesus's word. Even today there are people who are healed by Jesus in India in mass crusades who do not yet know He is the Son of God, but once they are healed by Him, they come to realize He is the Son of God. The healing is a sign that directs to the source of salvation, Jesus Christ. I have friends who minister to Muslims, Buddhists, and other non-Christian groups, and when they are healed in His name, they come to saving faith in Him.

**Blind man in John 9.** In John 9, we see another example of someone being healed without knowing Jesus's identity, or more correctly, without yet knowing that Jesus was the Son of Man, the Messiah. However, the man did have faith in Jesus as a righteous man who was from God and did God's will (see John 9:30-33). He still was healed by his faith. Even though he did not have a full understanding of who Jesus was, he had faith to obey what Jesus told him to do. In John's Gospel, these acts of obedience to the commands of Jesus are seen as acts of faith.

**Jairus's daughter.** The daughter of Jairus being raised from the dead is another example of someone being healed who did not have to exercise faith. It is noted that she could not have had faith for herself to be raised because she was, in fact, dead. Yet, the text indicates that faith or belief was a part of the story—not the girl's faith, but her father's (see Mark 5:23). When Jairus was told she had died, Jesus said to him, *"Don't be afraid, just believe"* (Mark 5:36). Jesus raised Jairus's daughter because he had exercised faith in Jesus's word to him.

**Lazarus.** Lazarus being raised from the dead is another example of a healing irrespective of the person's faith. In this narrative, Jesus does speak of faith. He says to Mary, *"Did I not tell you that if you believed, you would see the glory of God?"* (John 11:40). Then Jesus gave a command that involved the people in the miracle—He asked them to move the stone. This was another act of obedience that was indicative of faith. Thus, these two resurrections (Jairus' daughter and Lazarus) involved the faith of family members prior to their resurrections.

**Healing of the multitudes.** It is true that the Pharisees did not exercise faith in Jesus, but there is no indication that any of them were among the healed among the multitudes (see Matt. 12:24). The summary passage in Matthew 14:34-36 suggests that the people who were bringing the afflicted and sick into the streets, that they might touch Jesus's clothes, heard the testimony of the others who were previously healed, thus receiving faith in their hearts to bring other afflicted individuals to Jesus.

The similar account in Matthew 15 of the people being brought to Jesus, laid at His feet, and who were healed also does not mention faith or doubt, but the fact that they came to Jesus in need of healing implies they had faith and were expecting to be healed.

Thus, while these examples do not necessarily prove there was faith on the part of those being healed, neither do they prove the absence of faith. The context, however, lends support to the conclusion that there was a level of faith on the part of those coming to Jesus to receive healing. Why else would they have come to Him to begin with?

## THE VITAL LINK OF HEALING AND FAITH

Even though miracles can take place, in some instances, apart from faith on the recipient's end, the Gospels make a clear case for how faith actually unlocks the supernatural—even in Jesus's ministry. One of the most shocking accounts of this is in Matthew 13:58, where we read that Jesus *did not do many miracles there because of their lack of faith.* Mark 6:5-6 also states, *"He could not do any miracles there, except lay His hands on a few sick people and heal them. And He was amazed at their lack of faith."* There are many such passages that link the miraculous, healing, and deliverance to faith.

In reference to Matthew 13:58, the commentator Adam Clarke said, "Faith seems to put the almighty power of God into the hands of men; whereas unbelief appears to tie up even the hands of the Almighty."[77] This reminds us of the biblical importance of faith. Such a concept is not some invention of the Word of Faith Movement or even some Charismatic doctrine—it is clearly unveiled to us in the Scriptures.

> *The Gospels make a clear case for how faith actually unlocks the supernatural.*

*The New Bible Commentary*, regarding Mark 6:1-6, states, "So even the Son of God could do no *miracles* there, apart from healing a few sick folk, humble enough and needy enough to believe in

Him. That does not mean that God's power is absolutely limited, but that God has chosen to act only in response to faith."[78]

## A GNOSTIC GOSPEL?

There is nothing in Scripture to substantiate the claim that any mention of faith, as recorded in the Gospels, was emphasized as metaphorical for spiritual healing. In other words, some look at the examples in Scripture—where someone received a miraculous healing by faith—and rather than accept it at face value, recognizing the importance of faith in appropriating the miraculous, they spiritually allegorize the example. They emphasize that the act of placing faith in Jesus to receive physical healing is merely illustrative for the ultimate act of faith, which is spiritual healing through salvation.

While spiritual salvation undeniably carries overwhelming importance, the belief that all acts of faith are allegorical, pointing only to spiritual healing, is nothing but a departure from the true gospel and is influenced by Gnostic thought, which taught that only the soul was of importance, while the body was of no value.

This perspective contradicts Jesus's mission statement of Luke 4:18-19:

> *The Spirit of the Lord is upon Me, because He has anointed Me to preach the gospel to the poor. He has sent Me to proclaim release to the captives, and recovery of sight to the blind, to set free those who are oppressed, to proclaim the favorable year of the Lord.* (NASB)

This ideology also contradicts 1 John 3:8, that *"the reason the Son of God appeared was to destroy the devil's work."* John's statement must be understood in light of Peter's acknowledgement of Jesus's work in Acts 10:38: *"How God anointed Jesus of Nazareth with the Holy Spirit and power, and how He went around doing good and healing all who were under the power of the devil, because God was with Him."*

We cannot make the classic hermeneutical mistake of reading cessationist sixteenth-century theology back into the first-century text. If we do this, we mistake the purpose for miracles as being evidentialrather than as being part of the gospel. Instead of being limited to simply proving doctrine, the miracles were part of the good news, signaling the inbreaking of the Kingdom of God. Miracles do not just confirm or prove the gospel; they are the gospel in action.

## HEALERS, TELEVANGELISTS, AND MONEY MONGERING

Associating the healing ministry with televangelism and a strong emphasis upon money is another *straw man* that we must directly confront. Are there some who have connected too closely healing with financial offerings? Yes, some have. Is this typical, or even normative of the movement? No, this is not typical.

> *Most of the healings and miracles done in Jesus's name around the world are not done for money or fame, but by poor, humble servants of God.*

Most of the great healing ministries I am aware of around the world have little emphasis upon money connected to healing. Like the New Testament, most of the healings and miracles done in Jesus's name around the world are not done for money or fame, but by poor, humble servants of God, some of whom are illiterate and poor.

## COMPLETE OR INCOMPLETE HEALINGS

I have heard some use the example of the demonized boy in Mark 9:14-29, and conclude that the boy was not delivered for *his* lack of faith, but instead for the disciples' lack of faith—thus producing an incomplete healing. This is true, in part. However, in reviewing the account, it is important to remember that just because the faith of the sick person was not highlighted in this case, faith as a whole was not disregarded. It was the disciples' faith that was important. This confirms that the faith of the person ministering healing is also important, not just that of the recipient.

> *Healing, in many cases, is progressive. Just because it does not manifest completely and instantly does not give us reason to completely negate God's will to heal today.*

Regardless of the "faith" issue presented in this context, we see that because of the disciples' lack of faith they ended up with an incomplete healing. It does not remain this way, however. Jesus ends up stepping in and finishing the job, thus producing a complete healing.

Healing, in many cases, is progressive. Just because it does not manifest completely and instantly does not give us reason to completely negate God's will to heal today. Even Jesus was in a situation where He prayed for a blind man to receive healing, and it was progressive in nature (see Mark 8:22-26). In the end, however, it still ended up being a complete healing.

There is no such thing as the "golden-age of the church" that many have devised, where *all* healings were immediate and complete during the initial establishment of the church age. As we just examined, even Jesus Himself participated in a progressive miracle with the blind man in Mark 8. Likewise, there was no era where the apostles had a 100-percent success rate with the miracles they performed. We see that Paul had to leave Trophimus sick in Miletus (see 2 Tim. 4:20), and Epaphroditus almost died while with Paul (see Phil. 2:27).

It is true that many healings in the church today are not complete, yet many *are* complete. It is also true that for many in the healing ministry, the healings often take more than a single prayer or command. This is part of living in the "now-not yet" reality of the Kingdom of God. Healings today are signs of the inbreaking of the Kingdom, pointing to the day when it is fully consummated, and when all who are in Christ will be healed completely.

## HEALINGS AND MIRACLES TODAY!

God is still performing healings and miracles today. While on Global Awakening mission trips, we have teams that have spent thousands of dollars to be able to travel in order to pray for the sick. They receive nothing financial in return. We encourage the team to write up their reports of the healings they witnessed the night they happen because the details can become vague, especially with so many healings taking place, making it hard to remember them all. We even suggest using a small recorder after a significant healing to help remember the details.

In addition, we often have doctors on the teams who record the healings they experienced as they prayed in Jesus's name. The fact that they are doctors should provide another layer of credibility to the medical merits of the reports of healing and miracles. The fact that we had a brain research scientist and a psychiatrist ministering on trips who wrote about the healings should bring additional credibility.

Some find fault with healing ministers for having prearranged meetings for healing, noting that Jesus's healings were spontaneous. This was not always true. Sometimes they laid the people in the path of where Jesus was going to be coming in order that He might touch them. This line of argument is inconsistent, making one standard for healing and another standard for evangelism.

Critics of healing do not charge Billy Graham for conducting a form of evangelism that is programmed rather than spontaneous. That being said, most of the time healings *do* happen spontaneously for believers as they go about their lives. That is one of the reasons for training all Christians in how to recognize how the gifts of the Spirit operate in their lives. Without this knowledge, most of the spontaneous opportunities are missed. Likewise, these bizarre arguments for "scheduled healing meetings" could also be leveled against holding services on Sunday mornings where the gospel is preached to the lost. One is no more alien to the Bible than the other.

I know some people believe that if certain healers could actually do what they claim, disease would be completely eradicated in countries in the developing world and entire hospitals would be cleared out. Just like Jesus, these men and women would have the power to completely overthrow all matters of disease in whatever regions they visited.

First, the only time Jesus visited what would be similar to a hospital was the pool of Bethesda where He only healed one person and then walked out. Second, nowhere in the New Testament does it say that Jesus cured diseases in an entire country, or even an entire region. This is once again the enlightenment golden-age mentality that goes beyond the Scriptures.

# HEALING, THE GOSPEL, AND THE KINGDOM OF GOD

### An Evidential View of Miracles

When we view the purpose of miracles to be *evidential*, we believe that signs and wonders exist to validate true doctrine. After all, they validated the apostles who wrote the New Testament. The problem with this line of argument is that only very few of the apostles wrote Scripture—John, James, Peter, and Paul, whose qualifications would not fit the requirements of Acts 1.[79]

### The Purpose of Healing and Miracles

Because the real purpose of healing and miracles is to express the gospel, they are part of the gospel, and, as such, this function requires that they continue until the second coming of Jesus when the gospel will no longer need to be preached.[80]

The gospel is the gospel of the Kingdom, which includes the inbreaking of God's power to heal and deliver. Simple people with simple faith can be used to work miracles. People who only have an elementary understanding of doctrine, or, in some points, are incorrect in their doctrine, can also be used to administer God's healing power.

> *Miracles do not confirm the messengers; they confirm the gospel.*

Miracles do not authenticate doctrine. Instead, miracles point out the good news of a loving God who has power to help poor and often uneducated, illiterate people, and who are sick or demonized. The miracles express the gospel and are part of the gospel. The miracles do not confirm the messengers; they confirm the gospel.[81]

# WAS HEALING UNIQUE TO JESUS AND THE TWELVE APOSTLES?

First, Jesus did not intend for His ministry and that of the disciples to be unique when it came to the ministry of healing. Jesus said in John 14:12, *"I tell you the truth, anyone who has faith in Me will do what I have been doing. He will do even greater things than these, because I am going to the Father."*

There are scholars who see the commissioning of the twelve and the seventy-two as paradigmatic for the commissioning of the believers in the Great Commission of Matthew 28:18-20.[82] Mark 16:19 indicates the Lord was confirming His word by the signs that accompanied it. It is important to note once again that the confirmation was of the Word of God, not the apostles themselves.

The disciples remained in Jerusalem when the other Christians were scattered due to the persecution that was associated with Stephen. These unnamed disciples—not the apostles—also experienced the power of God for miracles and healing when they preached the gospel to the Gentiles in Antioch (see Acts 11:19-26). Luke uses the Jewish euphemism *"the hand of the Lord was with them"* to express the supernatural power of God that accompanied the gospel presentation (Acts 11:21 NKJV). Thus, healing was not the domain of the apostles only.

This is the position Jesus held. He did not limit healing to the apostles. He made it possible for anyone to be used in healing, though not all would have a gift of healing, and not all would be noted as a worker of miracles (see 1 Cor. 12:28).

Jesus said that anyone who believed in Him would be able to do what He had been doing, and even greater things than these could the believer do. These words of Jesus do not fit the view of the miracles and healings being limited to the apostles to prove correct doctrine. No, the purpose is noted in the next verse, which reads, *"And I will do whatever you ask in My name, so that the Son may bring glory to the Father"* (John 14:13).

Instead of exclusively authenticating correct doctrine, healings and miracles and other gifts of the Spirit, express the gospel. They are part of the good news that the Kingdom of God has come. They are expressions of the presence and power of the Kingdom. They are the means by which the Father receives glory.

## Summary

Divine healing is not simply an evidential proof, validating either the ministry of the early apostles or confirming that the doctrine they were preaching was correct. Healing and miracles actually extend the gospel, demonstrating the present Kingdom rule of Jesus over disease, affliction, and malady.

## Power Principles

1.  Healing and miracles do not simply offer proof that the first apostles were preaching correct doctrine; instead, they validate the actual gospel message.

2.  Faith plays an integral role in administering or receiving supernatural healing. Even though there are some examples, in both Jesus's day and our own, of people who received healing without demonstrating faith, the common key to experiencing the healing power of God is through placing one's faith in Christ, the Healer.

3. One does not need to be an author of Scripture or compiler of Bible doctrine to operate in supernatural ministry. There are several examples (in the Gospels and throughout the New Testament) of those who moved in powerful signs and wonders, healing the sick, who did not make any type of contribution to authoring the New Testament canon.

4. It is not scriptural to believe in a "golden age of healing," where every single person whom both Jesus and His disciples prayed for received instant, complete healing. Some would argue that this golden age took place during the life of Jesus and, perhaps, the book of Acts. However, even Jesus had at least one case of a progressive healing.

*Part Three*

# THE DISTINGUISHING MARKS OF A WORK OF THE SPIRIT OF GOD

*Five keys, based on the classic writings of Jonathan Edwards, that help evaluate an authentic work of the Holy Spirit.*

I believe Jonathan Edwards's work is a great source for developing discernment. In order to have a better understanding of Edwards and his perspective on the supernatural power of the Spirit, it is important to know what was going on in his own family, especially with his wife, Martha.

Martha experienced being overcome by the Spirit many times, sometimes for hours on end, unable to remain standing and often having to be taken to bed where she sometimes enjoyed hours of the joyful bliss of God. She was one frequently taken with these "emotional outbursts."[83]

In order to discern the spirits at work here, Edwards would ask five questions: 1) Does the work exalt the true Christ? 2) Does it oppose worldliness? 3) Does it point people to the Scriptures? 4) Does it elevate the truth? 5) Does it produce love for God and others? These are all drawn from 1 John 4:2-8, and we will explore each one in the next four chapters.

Before moving forward, however, it is worth reviewing the passage that Edwards derives his *distinguishing marks* from:

> *This is how you can recognize the Spirit of God: Every spirit that acknowledges that Jesus Christ has come in the flesh is from God, but every spirit that does not acknowledge Jesus is not from God. This is the spirit of the antichrist, which you have heard is coming and even now is already in the world.*
>
> *You, dear children, are from God and have overcome them, because the One who is in you is greater than the one who is in the world. They are from the world and therefore speak from the viewpoint of the world, and the world listens to them. We are from God, and whoever knows God listens to us; but whoever is not from God does not listen to us. This is how we recognize the Spirit of truth and the spirit of falsehood.*
>
> *Dear friends, let us love one another, for love comes from God. Everyone who loves has been born of God and knows God. Whoever does not love does not know God, because God is love.* (1 John 4:2-8)

To bring some further clarity to Edwards's method of discerning the spirits, I would have stated the *five marks* in the following manner from the same passage:

- Does the work acknowledge the incarnation of God in Jesus Christ?
- Does the person live a victorious Christian life or a defeated life?

- Does the work lead to a Christian worldview based upon the Bible or to a non-Christian worldview that diverges from the Bible? (The sin of unbelief is worse than sexual sin, according to Jesus's warning to Capernaum comparing it to Sodom and stating that Capernaum's judgment would be worse than Sodom's.)

- Does the work cause believers to listen to (obey, observe, do) the apostolic witness and commands in the Scriptures?

- Does this work produce love for others, especially those in Christ?

The remainder of this section will examine what happens when an individual uses Edwards's five marks, applying them to a move of the Holy Spirit.

*Chapter 8*

# DOES IT EXALT THE TRUE CHRIST?

*This is how you can recognize the Spirit of God: Every*
*spirit that acknowledges that Jesus Christ has come in*
*the flesh is from God, but every spirit that does not*
*acknowledge Jesus is not from God. This is the spirit*
*of the antichrist, which you have heard is coming and*
*even now is already in the world.* —1 JOHN 4:2-3

One of the hallmarks of false teaching is that it manipulates and distorts the truth about Christ. Is this not what cessationism has done to Christ and His gospel? Is this Jesus a limited Savior, and not the complete and full Savior the Scripture represents?

## IS THIS THE JESUS OF SCRIPTURE?

Cessationism does not see Jesus Christ as the same yesterday, today, and forevermore (see Heb. 13:8). Instead, the Jesus some present today is only concerned about the souls of people and about getting people forgiven so they can go to heaven. While this is

121

absolutely essential, we limit both the gospel and the Author of the gospel when we embrace a theology where the soul, or the spirit, is *all* that the gospel includes.

The Jesus of the Gospels was a greater Savior, who not only saved from sin, but from the consequences of sin—this included demonic torment, sickness, and disease. This is a much more holistic understanding of the work of Christ, not diminishing His work by limiting it to forgiveness and salvation alone, but expanding it to include forgiveness and salvation, while also including healing, deliverance, and the baptism with the Holy Spirit.[84]

His gospel is the gospel of the Kingdom (see Matt. 24:24), not redacted to the gospel of forgiveness. The Kingdom is greater than forgiveness, though it includes forgiveness. Forgiveness is an absolutely essential prerequisite to *entering* the Kingdom of God.

> *The Jesus of the Gospels was a greater Savior, who not only saved from sin, but from the consequences of sin.*

When we start to approach the gospel more holistically, some will accuse such a perspective of limiting the saving power of Jesus, while making healing, miracles, and other such items the front-and-center emphasis. Jesus's atonement at Calvary is non-negotiable. He is the only way to the Father, and there is no means of entry into the Kingdom of God but through the way of Jesus Christ, and receiving forgiveness for our sins through His redemptive work.

The problem takes place when we preach a gospel of forgiveness without including the *rest of the story*. In other words, many preach a gospel of forgiveness—which clearly tells people the way of entry into the Kingdom of God—without giving them appropriate follow-up once they have properly entered in. As mentioned, forgiveness is essential in order to make the first step *into* the Kingdom, but one thing that is sadly lacking in the body of Christ today is discipleship. Discipleship is missing when there is negligence to preach a holistic gospel.

## THE VICTORIOUS, CONQUERING CHRIST

Jesus is the Savior of sinners and the Son of God. Yes, all Charismatics would agree with this statement. Yet, it is a view of Jesus Christ that is too limited. To understand the work of Jesus on the cross as being exclusive to the substitutionary atonement view of the cross is to limit His work and diminish His glory and greatness. We need to have an honest confrontation with the full measure of what the cross actually made available to believers throughout all centuries.

> *Jesus on the cross is so great that it takes more than one understanding of the atonement to fully comprehend what He has done for us.*

Jesus on the cross is so great that it takes more than one understanding of the atonement to fully comprehend what He has done for us. I strongly believe in substitutionary atonement, the great exchange of mankind's sin for God's righteousness. It is the foundation and basis for us to be able to approach the throne of God boldly in our time of need (see Heb. 4:16).

However, the *kerygma*, the gospel, did not just focus on Jesus's death; it also focused on His resurrection, ascension, and pouring out of the New Covenant Spirit, the Holy Spirit. This understanding of the cross, known as Christus Victor, was the predominant understanding of the work of Jesus for the first eight hundred to a thousand years of the church.[85] Jesus is victor over death, demons, and disease. The gospel had impact for the present life, not just life after death.

Both of these understandings of the work of Jesus are needed to fully understand the nature of the gospel.

## TAKING THE GREAT COMMISSION LITERALLY

When it comes to fully expressing the Great Commission mandate, it is here that continuationists often believe that they are following Scripture most literally.

> *Then Jesus came to them and said, "All authority in heaven and on earth has been given to Me. Therefore go and make disciples of all nations, baptizing them in the name of the Father and of the Son and of the Holy Spirit, and teaching them to obey everything I have commanded you. And surely I am with you always, to the very end of the age."* (Matthew 28:18-20)

Continuationists believe the Great Commission is looking back to the paradigmatic passages of the commissioning of the twelve and the seventy-two. In other words, the model that Jesus gave when He commissioned the twelve and the seventy-two is the blueprint that we are to be following today. This is our paradigm for completing the Great Commission.

The second part of the Great Commission—*"and teaching them to obey everything I have commanded you"*—means that Christians are to continue to obey what Jesus emphasized to His disciples, with healing and deliverance being at the top, or at least near the top, of the list. Loving each other would also be near the top. While there is rightly an emphasis on walking in love toward another, there should likewise be a focus for us to all operate in the expressions of supernatural power that Jesus taught and modeled.

## JESUS, THE SPIRIT, AND THE KINGDOM

The Charismatic Movement, in its best representation, understands the community of the Trinity, how the Father points to Jesus, Jesus points to the Father, the Spirit points to the Son, and the Son points to the Spirit. It is this Trinitarian understanding of God, where there is mutual dependence upon the others and the mutual pointing beyond self to the others, that is appreciated.

Jesus's name is a means of having the authority and power to continue the works of Jesus by the Holy Spirit. The Holy Spirit is the *parakletos*, the One called to our side and who is exactly like Jesus, even as Jesus was exactly like His Father. The Holy Spirit is the Teacher who reminds us of Jesus's teachings—not just His ethical teachings, but also His commands to heal and deliver. The Holy Spirit is the seal and sign of the New Covenant. *He is the Spirit of the New Covenant.*

Obeying Jesus's teaching is not limited to doctrine or ethical implications; rather, it is much more than that. It also includes the emphasis of continuing His works and His deeds, especially His healing and miracles.[86]

When we limit the "work" of Jesus to salvation from damnation, we limit the scope of His teaching and instruction. While salvation from damnation is certainly true and a most important truth, it is not a full biblical understanding of the work of Jesus. Limiting the work of Jesus to salvation and not extending it to include the advancing of the Kingdom of God is a serious error.

In advancing the Kingdom of God, Jesus healed, cast out demons, prophesied, and ministered in other supernatural ways.

This was the message of the Kingdom—the good news that the Kingdom of God had dawned and broken out among mankind.

Jon Ruthven points out how central the Kingdom message was to the work of Jesus by asking five questions:

1. What is it that the New Testament says that Jesus came to do?

2. What does He actually spend His time doing?

3. What does Jesus tell His disciples to do?

4. What is it that they actually spend their time doing?

5. What is the reader of the New Testament (the "disciple of the disciples") expected to do?[87]

In answering these questions, Ruthven proves that a limited understanding of the work of Christ is flawed, and, as such, if followed, would deprive Jesus of His glory. One of the primary ways Jesus is glorified is through His disciples continuing His Kingdom works until He returns.[88] They are able to do this due to the New Covenant Spirit poured out upon the church.

## JESUS SPEAKS ON THE HOLY SPIRIT

It is true that the Spirit is to speak of Jesus, but it is also true that Jesus spoke about the Holy Spirit with great frequency. The New Testament has a 40-percent ratio of how often Spirit is used in comparison to how often Jesus is used. Let me explain what I mean.

New Testament writers reference Jesus 1,225 times and reference the Spirit 487 times in the New International Version. When the writings are limited to Acts through Revelation, the ratio becomes 75 percent. Jesus is referenced 362 times between Acts and Revelation, and the Spirit is referenced 272 times. When the Gospels, Acts, and the apocalyptic Revelation are excluded, then the ratio becomes 273 references to Jesus and 181 references to the Spirit for a 66 percent ratio. Because the Holy Spirit is the source for the inspiration of the Bible, it becomes obvious that He is not reluctant to refer to Himself in His Book.

Western theology tends to focus on the distinction between the persons of the Trinity, whereas Eastern theology and the upper room discourse focus more on the unity of the Trinity. If we see Jesus, then we see the Father (see John 14:9).

The term "another counselor," taken from John 14:16, means another just like Jesus who is called to our side to help us in our time of need. Just as Jesus was exactly like the Father, the Spirit is exactly like the Son.

What do Jesus's words mean when He says, *"But you know Him, for He lives with you and will be in you"* (John 14:17)? Is this not a reference to Himself, and yet somehow mysteriously also pointing to the Holy Spirit? *"Lives with you"* is the historical Jesus and *"will be in you"* is Jesus by means and power of the Holy Spirit.

Jesus also begins to explain how it is possible for Him to live "in our hearts" in John 14:20: *"On that day you will realize that I am in My Father, and you are in Me, and I am in you."* In what manner is Jesus in us? Is it not by the unity of the Trinity, by means of the Holy Spirit? Again in John 14:23, Jesus said, *"If anyone loves Me, he will obey My teaching. My Father will love him, and We will come to him and make Our home with him."* Now it is not only Jesus who is in us; both the Father and the Son are making their dwelling place in us. How is this possible? It is by the Holy Spirit.

# THE FRUIT OF "DOING" AND THE FRUIT OF "BEING"

Jesus says, "*I tell you the truth, anyone who has faith in Me will do what I have been doing. He will do even greater things than these, because I am going to the Father*" (John 14:12). In context, the "doing" Jesus referred to is the healings, deliverances, and miracles. One could call these works the "fruit of doing," versus what Paul discusses in Galatians as the "fruit of being."

It is important to note that the fruit of Galatians 5 is the fruit of "being," which deals with ethical characteristics, while Jesus is describing the fruit, or resulting actions, of those who do the same works that He has been doing. Both the fruit of doing and the fruit of being are important. It is also important to note how this fruit of doing, on the part of Jesus's disciples, is what brings glory to both the Father and the Son.

> *Now it is not only Jesus who is in us; both the Father and the Son are making their dwelling place in us. How is this possible? It is by the Holy Spirit.*

In John 14:13, Jesus continues to say, "*I will do whatever you ask in My name, so that the Son may bring glory to the Father. You may ask Me for anything in My name, and I will do it.*" The Trinity is working together for the purpose of extending glory to one another.

John 15:5-8 expresses this unity of the Trinity as Jesus states,

> *I am the vine; you are the branches. If a man remains in Me and I in him, he will bear much fruit; apart from Me you can do nothing. If anyone does not remain in Me, he is like a branch that is thrown away and withers; such branches are picked up, thrown into the fire and burned. If you remain in Me and My words remain in you, ask*

*whatever you wish, and it will be given you. This is to My Father's glory, that you bear much fruit, showing your-selves to be My disciples.*

How is Jesus to remain in us other than by the power and indwelling person of the Holy Spirit? Is this not what He is referring to? The secret to bearing much fruit in verses 5 and 8 is remaining in Jesus and Jesus remaining in the believer. What is important to note here is the teaching that we are to *remain in* is not limited to doctrinal and ethical aspects, but it is also referring to doing the works that Jesus did.

The Greek word translated *teaching* (see Matt. 28:20) in the NIV is *rhema* or word. It is a freshly spoken word for the occasion, as well as the body of Jesus's commandments. Dr. Ruthven has written power-fully about the need to include moving in the gifts of the Spirit, doing what Jesus did by the power of the Holy Spirit, as part of discipleship.[89]

## THE FOCAL POINT: JESUS CHRIST

In the end, the Holy Spirit will speak of Jesus. Jesus will speak of the Holy Spirit. The Holy Spirit will also speak of Himself in the Scriptures, because He is the Author of the Scriptures.

While celebrated, the gifts and blessings are not the focal point in the heart of the movement. Jesus is the center, just as He is the point of emphasis for the Holy Spirit. Char-

> *One key way that Jesus is exalted or glorified is through the working of the gifts of the Holy Spirit.*

ismatics desire, above all, for Jesus to be exalted. However, they understand that one key way that Jesus is exalted or glorified is through the working of the gifts of the Holy Spirit.

The Spirit glorifies and exalts Jesus by the signs and wonders, healings, and miracles that are worked through the Spirit's gifts and grace. This is an example of the Spirit and the Son working together, releasing a mutual glory. The Spirit receives glory as He functions in His position as the One who brings glory to the Son. Only in the Trinity can One receive glory by giving glory away, but because this exchange takes place in the context of the Godhead, such logic would make complete Kingdom sense.

Charismatics do not limit the work of Christ, or the scope of the cross. They fully acknowledge everything that Jesus did for us in His death, resurrection, ascension, and pouring out of the Spirit. They recognize the ongoing work of Jesus Christ in and through the Spirit to continue His mission and fulfill the great commission.

Finally, we corporately exalt the matchless power and all-sufficient authority of that one name—Jesus—before whom every knee must bow and every tongue confess, to the glory of God the Father.

## Summary

When answering the question of whether the true Christ is being exalted, we must ask, "Is our understanding of Jesus's atoning work limited, or is it vast?" The true Christ of the true cross overcame sin and also dealt with every consequence that sin produced in humanity. This includes disease, demons, torment, and other such ills. Jesus's complete provision at the cross has obtained victory over every one of these ills.

# Power Principles

1. Christ's work on the cross not only purchased forgiveness, making a way for one to enter the Kingdom of God and receive salvation, but also made victorious *power* available to every single person who has received the new birth and has become a citizen of the Kingdom of God.

2. The Holy Spirit and Jesus do not work independently of one another; the Spirit points to Jesus, and, likewise, Jesus points to the Spirit. It is the Holy Spirit who makes it possible for believers to be indwelt by Christ to begin with.

3. We exalt Jesus by taking the Great Commission literally, presenting a message of repentance and forgiveness, along with equipping believers to become effective followers and disciples of Jesus by doing the same works He did.

*Chapter 9*

# DOES IT OPPOSE WORLDLINESS?

*You, dear children, are from God and have overcome*
*them, because the One who is in you is greater than*
*the one who is in the world. They are from the world*
*and therefore speak from the viewpoint of the world,*
*and the world listens to them.* —1 JOHN 4:4-5

When exploring this issue of worldliness, it is important for us to
have a balanced understanding of sanctification. Our vision becomes
blurry when our understanding of worldliness and sanctification are
too narrow, focusing only on moral issues of sanctification—the
negative side—and spending little time emphasizing the positive
side and "what to do."

To remain exclusively focused on the negative, we leave people
powerless and directionless when it comes to following Jesus. To
oppose worldliness is not simply *not* to do certain things, but to
embrace a whole new perspective and approach to the Christian life.

## TRUE TESTS OF THE SPIRIT'S PRESENCE AND ACTIVITY

When evaluating a work of the Holy Spirit, some comment that
the different manifestations of the Spirit's work in someone's life

are not sufficient to produce holiness and to confirm the authentic power that God is at work. Phenomena that often occur in the Pentecostal, Charismatic, and Third Wave Movements include tongues, falling under the power, trances, prophecy, and feeling electricity. Scripture indicates that tongues, falling, trances, prophecy, and energy are all indicators of the Spirit's presence.

Critics would say that these unusual manifestations or demonstrations of power are insufficient examples of good "fruit," thus disproving the Holy Spirit's involvement in the activities taking place. The weakness of such an argument regarding sanctification and the work of the Spirit is in limiting the Spirit's work to the fruit of Galatians 5 while ignoring the fruit Jesus spoke of in John 14–16. In the previous chapter, we categorized these as the "fruit of doing" and the "fruit of being."

> *To oppose worldliness is not simply not to do certain things, but to embrace a whole new perspective and approach to the Christian life.*

In ignoring the fruit of doing and focusing only on the fruit of being, we fail to recognize that Jesus regarded the sin of unbelief to be more serious than the sin of homosexuality when He said it would be better for the people of Sodom than for the people of Capernaum who had seen His miracles and still would not believe (see Matt. 10:15; 11:23-24; Luke 10:12.).

Again, we cannot embrace an either/or paradigm when it comes to the Holy Spirit, making Him either an agent of power *or* of holiness. Remember, the Spirit's presence produces holiness, but it is also for power. It is truly a both/and situation—not holiness *or* power, but holiness *and* power.[90] The choice between fruit and gifts is an illegal choice—it is fruit *and* gifts not fruit *or* gifts. Sanctification is not only related to the fruit of Galatians 5, it is also related to the fruit of John 14 and 15—the fruit of being and doing are both important to the process of sanctification.

Being afraid to do what God commands is much greater than many define, and thus comprehend. It is not limited to moral and ethical behavior, but also to obeying the commissions of Jesus and bearing the fruit of doing.

The good works of Ephesians includes the works made possible only by the activity of the Holy Spirit. The fruit is dependent upon the work of the Holy Spirit. He gives revelatory gifts: words of knowledge, words of wisdom, prophecy, and discerning of spirits.

> *The Spirit's presence produces holiness, but it is also for power.*

These grace-enablements are used to create another gracelet, the grace-enabled gift of faith (see 1 Cor. 12:4-11).

This grace gift, in turn, helps to release the grace gifts of power: gifts of healing and working of miracles. The gracelet of tongues can also be used to build sensitivity, anointing, courage, and faith for the gifts of revelation that, in turn, release the key of faith for the power gifts.

How do these oppose worldliness, as defined by Edwards? When we possess a clear understanding of what the domain of satan includes, we recognize that worldliness, or the demonic system under the influence of satan, is not limited exclusively to sin and moral corruption. All of the enemy's works should be targets for destruction, as this was Jesus's mandate: *"the reason the Son of God appeared was to destroy the devil's work"* (1 John 3:8). This includes sin, yes, but it also includes disease, oppression, and other works of the evil one that have resulted from the impact of sin.

# IDENTIFY THE WORKS OF THE ENEMY

It is naive of us to solely equate the activity of satan to temptation and moral sins, especially sexual sin or greediness. Yet, there is strong evidence that the Bible also sees sickness and demonization as works of the enemy that also need to be overcome (see Luke 10:19).

Edwards notes that "when the spirit that is at work operates against the interests of satan's kingdom, which lies in encouraging and establishing sin, and cherishing men's worldly lusts; this is a true sign that it is a true, and not a false spirit." By this definition, when we see people being healed of their diseases, delivered from the demons, or raised from the dead, or when prisoners are visited and personal and systemic poverty is addressed, then we know that God is in our midst.

The true, powerful work of the Holy Spirit is being wrought in our midst as darkness is being driven out, for surely such things as were just listed above belong to satan's kingdom. It is vital that we do not maintain a perspective that is too limited when it comes to the work of Jesus or the works of satan.

I would have elaborated on this particular *mark* of a work of the Holy Spirit by asking this question: Does the person live a victorious Christian life or a defeated life? Based on the definition we were just exploring, victory and defeat have many faces. It is important for us to recognize this. Yes, we experience victory when we overcome temptation and resist sin. Likewise, we step into defeat when we cave in to temptation and yield to sin. However, these are not the only expressions of victory and defeat for the Christian.

Victory is also gained when we release the power of God over disease or the demonic and watch as the Holy Spirit pushes back those expressions of darkness. At the same time, we can experience defeat when sickness or strongholds are constantly getting the "upper hand" in our lives, and when we wrestle against them with no results—often, not aware of the authority we have received in Christ and the power that is dwelling within us in the person of the Holy Spirit.

## A COMMON CRITICISM

One could compile a "dirty laundry list" of Pentecostals and Charismatics, going back into the early 1900s and taking us right up to the twenty-first century, with the congressional investigation into several well-known Charismatic ministries. Based on this alleged "evidence," critics contend that Charismatics are more prone to fall into moral error and worldliness than other evangelicals.

For one to appropriately prove this point, however, they would need to provide scientific evidence of more wrongdoing in the Pentecostal/Charismatic world than in the evangelical/fundamentalist world. Apart from such evidence, the critic is guilty of purely extrapolating from anecdotal evidence with no real proof that the percentage of Pentecostals and Charismatics who fall into sexual sin or sins of greed is higher than such sins among evangelicals and fundamentalists.

Invariably, this line of criticism culminates with the prosperity gospel. Critics contend that faulty, mammon-driven doctrine actually feeds the moral unscrupulousness of the Charismatic Movement. Their reasoning would also suggest that people are often converted into Charismatic/Pentecostal Movements, not because of a legitimate salvation experience, but because they were enticed by false assurance of wealth, materialism, and worldliness.

This seems to be an attempt to deny the legitimacy of the numbers of people genuinely converted in these movements. Contrary to the opinion of some critics, there are many fast-growing Pentecostal and Charismatic Movements that do not embrace the popular understanding of the prosperity movement, thus leading to worldliness.

## IRIS MINISTRIES: AN EXAMPLE OF PURITY AND POWER

I am aware of such a movement in Mozambique that I think is one of the best representations of Christianity in the world. Drs. Rolland and Heidi Baker's ministry, Iris Ministries, definitely would not embrace the prosperity gospel. Iris has planted over 10,000 churches and has led over one million people to the Lord.

The Bakers represent a fine example of understanding the work of Christ in a way that does not limit His work to salvation, but believes in the work of the risen Savior, the One who baptizes with the Holy Spirit, and who is the Head of the church.

They began their work with just the two of them, but after being powerfully touched by the Holy Spirit during the Toronto Blessing, they went back and recruited twelve men. They built orphanages and followed a prophetic word that claimed, "God is going to give you the nation of Mozambique. The blind will see, the deaf will hear, the lame will walk, and the dead will be raised."

During the initial time in Mozambique after receiving this prophecy, many trials plagued the Bakers. It definitely did not look like the prophecy was coming to pass. In fact, it appeared to be the exact opposite. Heidi was diagnosed with multiple sclerosis, her husband had cerebral malaria, her daughter had malaria three times, her son was experiencing various trials, the government confiscated their orphanages, they lost 90 percent of their support, and they lost one million dollars of pledged donations. All of these things occurred within eighteen months of Heidi receiving the prophetic word.

In spite of the circumstances, however, Heidi was able to maintain faith in the prophetic word. If someone was to ask how she could sustain her faith in the prophecy, the answer is because of the power of God that instantly backed up the word. This power was so strong that it caused manifestations: crying, heat, sweat, energy that felt like electricity, laughter, and, at one point, the inability to move anything below her neck. It was this confirmation of power that enabled her to believe the prophecy when for the first eighteen months it appeared the opposite was happening.

Evidently, the Bakers hold to a holistic gospel. Iris Ministries digs wells for water, provides food for 10,000 children each day, helps build mud and rock churches, cares for cholera victims, buildings schools and clinics, and has worked on building a hospital and a university. They do not place an emphasis upon raising money, and they never solicit funds. They are truly the opposite of the carnal prosperity gospel. Yet, they do believe in healing, miracles, and supernatural provision, all while living a simple, humble lifestyle.

They are also not anti-intellectual people. Heidi has a Ph.D. from King's College London in systematic theology, and Rolland has a Doctor of Ministry degree from United Theological Seminary. They believe in presence evangelism (social gospel implications), presentation evangelism (personal gospel implications), and power evangelism (through signs and wonders). Their lives and ministry undeniably vindicates the continuationist position.

═══════════ *Summary* ═══════════

The Charismatic Movement is unjustly accused of promoting worldliness by focusing on more "fleshly" elements, such as signs, wonders, and manifestations, than on a spiritual emphasis. Such an accusation comes from a nearly Gnostic perspective, as the gospel is holistic in demonstration, both transforming one's interior spirit-man and delivering the same individual from demonic torment, disease, and other ills wrought by the effects of sin. While there are examples of Charismatics who have placed an exaggerated emphasis on worldly matters, namely, prosperity and fulfilling sensual desires, such are few and far between when measured beside the entire global collective of Charismatics.

═══════════ *Power Principles* ═══════════

1. The indwelling presence of the Holy Spirit enables a believer to walk in purity and power, holiness and supernatural demonstrations, such as healings, the prophetic, speaking in tongues, etc. Jesus never presented an "either/or" situation when it came to the gifts and fruit of the Spirit.

2. It is unfair to characterize the entire Charismatic Movement as "worldly" or exclusively pursuing sensual pleasures simply due to the few (but sadly, public and notable) examples of individuals and leaders who have been caught in moral compromise. When measured beside the greater body of Charismatics

worldwide, those who espouse a carnal prosperity message, or who have fallen into worldliness, represent a very small minority.

3. When it comes to resisting the kingdom of darkness and identifying the works of satan, we cannot exclusively limit our understanding to temptation and compromising moral boundaries. The same satan who tempts is also the one who afflicts. Just as Jesus was made manifest to destroy the works of the devil (see Acts 10:38; 1 John 3:8), so we have been authorized and anointed to identify these works, resist them, and ultimately, destroy them (see John 20:21).

*Chapter 10*

# DOES IT POINT PEOPLE TO THE SCRIPTURES?

*We are from God, and whoever knows God listens to us; but whoever is not from God does not listen to us. This is how we recognize the Spirit of truth and the spirit of falsehood.* —1 JOHN 4:6

We want to take this third mark slightly further. I am in no way belittling what Edwards provided as a tool to evaluate whether or not a movement is the authentic work of the Spirit. Truly, his five marks are exceptional tools of evaluation that will provide the body of Christ invaluable aid for time immemorial.

However, for Edwards's third test—Does it point people to the Scriptures?—I want to continue with this follow-up question: Does the work lead to a Christian worldview based upon the Bible or to a non-Christian worldview that diverges from the Bible?

## ARE WE BELITTLING THE BIBLE?

Critics of the contemporary move of the Spirit would comment on how people allegedly twist Scripture, adding their own ideas

143

and interpretations to it, thus branding their *false prophecies* as "revelation" or "insight" directly given by the Holy Spirit.

First, examples are once again rare and are of the minority of Charismatics. Two, the irony of this perspective is that cessationist critics are often guilty of this very thing—belittling the Scriptures—by twisting their meaning. They begin with an idea, that the work of the Spirit does not operate today as it did during the ministry of Jesus or the apostles, and that single driving perspective is what forms their interpretive stance of Scripture.

> *The same Jesus who gave us the Sermon on the Mount also told us that the miraculous works He performed we would also do.*

This is what causes them to ignore many passages that clearly and plainly indicate commands, such as in the Great Commission, *"And teaching them to obey everything I have commanded you"* (Matt. 28:20). We have already studied how Jesus's commands were not exclusively moral in nature, but they were also demonstrative. He did not propose a Christian experience where morality was upheld at the expense of power, or vice versa. The same Jesus who gave us the Sermon on the Mount also told us that the miraculous works He performed we would also do (see John 14:12). To simply ignore these clear statements, we run the risk of being dishonest with the text.

The Bible was not meant to only be a theological book, a historical book, or an ethics manual. It is all of these, but it is also a manual explaining how to work with the Holy Spirit to do the things Jesus did. We belittle Scripture when we view it one-dimensionally, and respond to it as such.

# THE HOLY SPIRIT AND THE REVELATION OF SCRIPTURE

Jesus explained that when the Holy Spirit came, one of His key functions would be to reveal Jesus's words to His followers. In context (John 13–17), the disciples were receiving Jesus's farewell address. Many of His words went beyond their natural understanding at the time, and it would not be until He died, rose again, and sent the Holy Spirit that some of His final instructions would start to make spiritual sense.

That being said, limiting the Holy Spirit's revealing of the words of Jesus to what is expressly stated in the New Testament is itself eisogesis rather than exegesis. This drastically limits the role of the Holy Spirit, both in how Jesus's words could be fulfilled and the time frame when they could be fulfilled.

This does not mean that Charismatics are expecting the Holy Spirit to move in ways that are outside of or contrary to the established perimeters of Scripture. Such an accusation is outlandish. All of the leaders I personally know in the Pentecostal or Charismatic Movements hold that the Bible is the basis for determining whether or not a revelation or illumination from the Holy Spirit is valid. If it contradicts the Bible, then it must be rejected.

The Bible itself, however, teaches that God spoke to the early church through dreams and visions, hearing the Lord speak to them directly through specific prophetic words, and sometimes combinations of these various ways of communication. Critics tend to believe that any communication or revelation that comes from beyond the Bible leads to disastrous ramifications, completely undermining the sufficiency of Scripture. This perspective is reading into Pentecostals and Charismatics something they do not believe in.

I do not know of any Pentecostals or Charismatics who believe that Holy Spirit communications can be or should be on an equal level of authority with the Bible. Instead, the ones I know believe all revelations from the Holy Spirit must be evaluated or judged by whether or not they conform to the Bible. They believe that the canon of Scripture has been closed. They contend that the Bible is sufficient, and that the Bible itself points to revelation beyond itself.

## What They Believe...

We cannot simply ignore the doctrinal statements of Pentecostals and Charismatics, all affirming their bold commitment to the uniqueness of the Bible and its sufficiency for doctrine and practice.[91] In fact, the Bible was delivered to its writers as they heard and discerned the divine voice of the Spirit.

Additionally, there are multiple examples of those who experienced God speaking to them in supernatural ways, but the result of these encounters was not their contribution to the authoritative canon of Scripture. In the New Testament, the Holy Spirit does not speak supernaturally simply to instruct and inspire the authors of Scripture. Some would say that God only spoke through unusual ways during these formative years of the church because He was using extraordinary means to communicate the truth of Scripture to its authors.

While it is true that the Spirit *did* communicate to the authors of Scripture in a supernatural manner, there are also examples of those who received a prophetic word to travel to a specific destination. In other cases, God used visions, dreams, and even trances to let His people know of significant shifts that were going to take place in His plan for salvation—namely, the trance He had Peter fall under, and then the vision He gave Peter of the sheet and the unclean animals, which signified the inclusion of the Gentiles into the unfolding redemptive agenda of God (see Acts 10–11). While this was always part of God's plan, He used a divine method to communicate it to His servant, Peter.

## THE SPIRIT IS STILL SPEAKING

Review the New Testament and you will witness a variety of instances where God spoke to His people directly and supernaturally. You would see this in how God spoke to Peter, Philip, Paul, Ananias, and John, and through angelic encounters, dreams, visions, prophecies, and direct words from the Holy Spirit. It is the Bible, the words of Jesus Himself, and the words that the apostle Peter preached on the day of Pentecost that emphasize the continued role of the Holy Spirit as the Spirit of the New Covenant.[92]

> *The same Holy Spirit who authored Scripture is still speaking to us today. We can trust His voice, for He will never contradict what He has spoken in the past.*

Remember, Jesus not only said that the Holy Spirit would remind us of what He had spoken, but *"He will not speak on His own; He will speak only what He hears, and He will tell you what is yet to come"* (John 16:13).

The same Holy Spirit who authored Scripture is still speaking to us today. We can trust His voice, for He will never contradict what He *has* spoken in the past. What we have recorded in the canon of Scripture are the timeless words directly inspired and authored by the Holy Spirit. He will never violate what He has said or give revelation that contradicts what has been written.

That said, He will surely give us increased understanding and clarity on what has *been* written. To claim absolute, final knowledge of every nuance of Scripture, even in a single theological subject, is beyond arrogant. Scripture is not expanding, because the canon is closed. However, our understanding of Scripture is ever developing, as the Holy Spirit leads us and guides us into all truth (see John 16:13).

The Word of God, the Scriptures themselves, reveal that God will continue to give us revelation until Jesus returns (see John 14–16; 1 Cor. 13:8). This was the position of the early church in their response to Montanism.[93] It is what the Bible actually teaches, not just for the apostolic period, but for all of church history.

## CAN WE MISS THE SPIRIT BUT KNOW THE BIBLE?

The Pharisees and religious leaders of Jesus's day were biblical scholars but missed the appearance of the Son of God. They knew the Scriptures but completely missed their point and rejected their function (see John 5:37-39).

As Dr. Ruthven points out, one of the reasons that these leaders missed Jesus was their cessationist position that the time of revelation had ended with the Old Testament.[94] Their version of the sufficiency of the Scriptures was detrimental to their ability to recognize and acknowledge Jesus. The cessationist version of the sufficiency of Scripture is detrimental to their ability to recognize and acknowledge the Holy Spirit.

## BIBLICAL REVELATION

It is actually a Charismatic paradigm that believes that scriptural revelation is the model for and invitation to expect the Lord Jesus to come to the believer through the power of the Holy Spirit. The Bible reveals God communicating His love for His people, which He does through revelation of directions for specific decisions: dreams, visions, prophecies, words of wisdom, insights into the will of God for healing—both physical and emotional—words of knowledge, prophecy, and impressions regarding words or Scripture.

Scripture portrays the early leaders of the church as people who were organically led by the Holy Spirit. It is not a rejection of the authority and sufficiency of Scripture to believe that the Word of God invites us, instructs us, and, yes, even models for us the expectation of experiencing the Father and the Son coming into us by the Holy Spirit, and the Son making known to us things He has received from the Father through revelatory communication via the Holy Spirit (see John 14–16). Intimacy with God includes God making known to us specific insights needed for either specific situations or specific persons who need a specific word from God. The scripture clearly reveals God communicating directly through His supernatural gifts.

> *Scriptural principles should not become the substitute for being led by His presence and voice.*

In summary, regarding the Spirit and the Scripture, the Bible never claims to gag God and to limit His sovereignty, but instead paints a picture of how He directs us in making decisions pertaining to personal directions. God can lead us and train us in holiness through the Scriptures, revealing His nature and will for our character, especially the fruit of Galatians 5:22-23.

Godly principles are important to know, however, scriptural principles should not become the substitute for being led by His presence and voice. The Scriptures actually teach that being filled with the Spirit not only produces the fruit of Galatians, the fruit of being, but also the fruit of John 14–16, the fruit of doing.

It must be remembered that both the fruit and the gifts are all the product of the Spirit's work in our lives. The Spirit's work is always a work of grace. Therefore, there is no place for pride, either for powerful gifts or for good fruit—both are the product of God's grace.

## Summary

God still speaks to His people today, and He communicates through a variety of unusual, extraordinary ways. The Bible describes such methods as dreams, visions, trances, and prophetic revelation. When God communicates to us in one of these supernatural ways, it is our responsibility to evaluate what was communicated by what is written in Scripture. The Word of God is the final standard of evaluation for measuring all alleged divine communication.

## Power Principles

1.  God is still speaking to His people today through a variety of different, New Testament means, including dreams, visions, revelation, trances, prophecies, etc.

2.  The same Holy Spirit who *spoke* to the authors of Scripture and inspired the writing of the biblical texts will never violate what has already been written and recorded. Scripture is the believer's final standard and authority for judging dreams, visions, revelations, and prophetic words.

3. Any revelation that a person claims to have received from the Holy Spirit is not purposed to add to or subtract from what has been presented as canonized Scripture. Rather, Scripture evaluates the legitimacy of the revelation received.

4. Revelation is not about adding to what is recorded in Scripture; it is about unveiling new understanding and clarity of *what has been written* to the believer, enabling him or her to walk in new levels of obedience, purity, and power, becoming a more effective disciple of the Lord Jesus Christ.

# Chapter 11

# DOES IT ELEVATE THE TRUTH AND PROMOTE LOVE FOR GOD AND OTHERS?

I have combined Jonathan Edwards's two concluding *marks* in this single chapter, as I firmly believe that a commitment to truth and experience of the Spirit are not on opposing ends of the spectrum. Biblical truth should lead us into experiences with the Holy Spirit, and these encounters will produce an increased love for both God and people.

## A THEOLOGY OF ENCOUNTER

Doctrine and experience are not at odds with each other, as if one had to pick either doctrine *or* experience. The truth is that they should go hand in hand. What we read about in Scripture is not simply

> *Doctrine and experience are not at odds with each other.*

for the purpose of acquiring more head knowledge. Rather, the Bible should become a blueprint and manual, fueling our expectation for what is possible in a life indwelt by God.

Time after time, we are implored to be doers of the Word, not hearers only (see James 1:22). This is a summons, not to a purely academic or theological faith, but rather to an experiential faith. This is your biblical invitation to a life of encounter with God.

Academics and theology are beneficial, but if these simply lead to one who becomes "puffed up" with knowledge but does not bear the fruit of a discipled life wholly surrendered to Jesus, increased knowledge does little good for this individual. We are transformed through encountering Christ, not just reading about Him. The words that we read about Jesus are purposed to usher us into transformative, "glory-to-glory" encounters with Him, where we take on His attitudes, character, and nature in greater dimensions (see 2 Cor. 3:18).

> *We do not need to pit the Word of God against the works of God.*

It is actually the biblical experiences that affect the hermeneutic, causing one to move from both liberal theology and dispensational cessationist theology into embracing the continuationist position. A theology of encounter makes the Scriptures come to life before one's very eyes.

When someone sees two brothers' blind eyes open, as did a professor who specialized in brain research at Washington University, it becomes difficult to remain a cessationist. This professor was a member of a Presbyterian church, and he had been discipled as a cessationist, but he could not, with intellectual honesty, continue as a cessationist after a trip with Global Awakening to Brazil where he saw many healings and a few miracles.[95]

# RHEMA VERSUS LOGOS?

We do not need to pit the Word of God against the works of God. There is the *logos* word of God, and the *rhema* word of God. The *logos* does not teach there will be an elimination of the *rhema*; instead, the *logos* teaches the continuation of the *rhema*. *Logos* also teaches that the *rhemas* are one of the main ways God creates faith that releases the supernatural power of God through the gifts of His Holy Spirit. This was the pattern of Jesus—He did what the Father showed Him and He said what the Father spoke to Him. This seeing and hearing was communicated to Jesus via the Holy Spirit (see John 5:19; 8:28).

> **Faith is the key to the supernatural.**

Faith is the key to the supernatural. This faith is a gift, and this gift is often created by the operation of other revelatory gifts. The gift of faith is the agent that releases the power gifts of healing or miracles. Thus, the miracle or healing begins in grace, a grace of revelation that leads to the grace of faith that releases the grace of power to affect the miracle or healing by the energy of God.

Though it is true that the Bible says we are healed by faith, it is true in the sense that it is faith that releases the energy of God, which is the primary agent or cause of healing, with faith being the secondary agent or cause of healing.[96]

# OUR FINAL AUTHORITY

The Word of God is also our supreme rule for practices: how to pray for the sick, how to do deliverance, how to evangelize, how to plant churches, how to oversee churches, how to prophesy, how to worship, etc. When we honor the Word of God with our practices as well as our doctrine, we must be committed to the continuationist position of living a lifestyle open to the inbreaking of the grace and gifts of the Holy Spirit that take us beyond the natural into a biblical-type experience of the supernatural.

Furthermore, we must not only be concerned for the honor of God, we must also be concerned for the *glory of God*. Let us remember that the number one way the Father and the Son receive glory, biblically speaking, is through the fruit of the works of His disciples—supernatural works made possible by His grace and gracelets.[97] This is the fruit of doing that I have argued for throughout this book.

Unfortunately, many cessationists do not deal with the biblical scholars who have charismatic experiences, or who embrace revivals, prophecies, healings, and miracles, preferring instead to attack those without a solid theological training.[98]

## SPIRIT AND TRUTH

It is time for us to abandon the ridiculous Charismatic caricature, where all adherents are portrayed as "wild enthusiasts" and "wild fanatics" who would obviously meet Jonathan Edwards's disapproval (according to this skewed definition). This incorrect representation of the Charismatic Movement is unfair. Not all, not even the majority, of Charismatics are wild enthusiasts or wild fanatics. By some cessationist standards, Jonathan Edwards's own wife would be judged a wild enthusiast. Yet, Jonathan Edwards did not disapprove of her falling under the power, being overcome with joy and rapture, or being taken to bed sometimes for hours under the sweet influence of the Holy Spirit.

Charismatics are not trading in truth for experience. On the contrary, when we do not allow the emphasis of the Scriptures to be our emphasis in life, we are treating the Scriptures in an insufficient manner. The primary understanding of faith requires personal revelation that we must obey.[99]

Likewise, Charismatics and Pentecostals do not disdain or neglect the truth of Scripture. Instead, their view of the Bible is not to reduce it to a historical or theological book, but approach it as the living Word of God. Rather than being limited to a historical or theological book—it is that and *more*—it is also the practical training manual for everyday discipleship. In fact, the truth presented throughout Scripture is the discipleship training manual for the church on how to live lives that produce fruit—fruit of Galatians 5 and John 14–16.

When all is said and done, biblical principles should never become a substitute for the privilege of knowing and being led by the Holy Spirit's presence. The truth of these scriptural principles undeniably demand adherence and obedience, but we must understand that such obedience leads to walking in the supernatural power of the Spirit. Embracing this perspective on biblical truth is by no means a distortion or aberration.

Once more, personal revelation—received from the Holy Spirit—is not sought because the Bible is insufficient. The Bible actually teaches that personal revelation is an end result of the work of Jesus. Because of His death, resurrection, and ascension, the Holy Spirit has been poured out. He is the Source of the personal revelation that is the way believers respond to God (i.e. faith), which is the essence of the meaning of New Testament and Old Testament faith.

The Bible does not give us specific directions for our lives, but it does show us how the Holy Spirit led the New Testament church—through dreams, visions, prophecy, and the word of the Lord coming to believers via the Holy Spirit. This is how the Bible shows

Christians were led in their personal lives, and the same Scripture gives no indication that God's methods for communicating with His people have changed. The New Testament itself emphasizes such supernatural direction. This is not "downplaying biblical truth" because one prefers experience. Instead, this is highlighting the very emphasis of Scripture, as Ruthven has pointed out.[100]

God desires to communicate with His people and lead them every single day of their lives. Jesus made provision for every single person who received His atoning work to be filled with the Spirit of God.

> *The same Spirit at work in the early church is at work today.*

The same Spirit at work in the early church is at work today. He has not changed strategies. Scripture exposes us to the nature and character of God, but also the means and methods of the Holy Spirit for exchanging information with His people.

## THE NATURE OF WORSHIP—LOVING GOD

When we obey the truth of Scripture, it leads us to not only enjoy a supernatural Christian life—where we walk in both the fruit and the gifts of the Spirit, demonstrating the compassion *and* power of Jesus—but it intensifies our love for both God and people. Our love for God is expressed in the context of worship, while our love for people is expressed through many of the ways we have studied so far—releasing healing, deliverance, a timely prophetic word, etc.

Some would argue that worship looks a certain way, and that the Charismatic expression lacks in truth, sound theology, order, and reverence. Such a perspective is not based on Scripture, but rather on preference. When giving perimeters for what *demonstrative praise and worship* should look like, the Bible tells us to shout to the Lord,[101] to dance before the Lord,[102] bow before the Lord,[103] lift our hands to the Lord,[104] and to worship in Spirit and in truth.[105] Worship is not just a sober-minded intellectual activity; it is a whole body experience that also includes the mind.

During my last pastorate, I would tell our congregation that we did not allow body racks in the foyer. They would give me a puzzled look. Then I would explain, "We do not have body racks in the foyer where you can zip out of your body, hang it on a rack, and then let your two-and-a-half pound brain float in to rest on a seat to simply contemplate God and doctrine."

Psalms is the worship book of the Bible and it has many commands to worship in ways that involve our bodies as well as our minds. Worship that is both in spirit and in truth will involve our volition, our affections, our body movements, and our contemplation. Declarative praise and intimate worship that involves prostrating, bowing, lifting hands, clapping, dancing, shouting, singing, and being still at times, are actually commanded in the Bible. King David and the other psalmists would surely be branded today as being "wildest enthusiasts" and "wild fanatics."

## Summary

Bible truth and supernatural experiences are not at odds with each other. In fact, truth leads to encounter. When we obey the truth of Scripture, not merely being content to hear it or read about it, we become true disciples of Jesus Christ. This means we manifest both His character and His power as we step out on what Scripture reveals and follow its instructions. As a result, our exposure to truth develops us into disciples who walk in God's supernatural power, not for the purpose of spectacle, but to demonstrate compassion and love to those in need. If the truth of Scripture does not lead us to an increased love for both God and people, we are simply accumulating knowledge and becoming more and more puffed up.

# *Power Principles*

1. Truth and experience are not at theological odds with each other; truth actually ushers us into the place of encounter. When we step out on what Jesus commands and reveals in Scripture (truth), we position ourselves to demonstrate both His character and power (experience). The problem takes place when we pursue experiences that are out of line with the truth.

2. Truth is not given to us for the purpose of acquisition and accumulation of knowledge. There are many who have theology degrees and who are not actively cultivating the character of Jesus in their lives, nor are they experiencing His power in their ministries.

3. If knowledge is our end-goal, we will become puffed-up and prideful. If Kingdom transformation of self and of others is our end-goal, then truth will become a launching pad for us to operate in the power of the Holy Spirit.

*Part Four*

# EXPERIENCE THE HOLY SPIRIT TODAY

*Understanding who the Holy Spirit is, activating His power in your life as a citizen of the Kingdom, and answering some key questions about His supernatural activity.*

We cannot simply limit the Holy Spirit's role to initiating and orchestrating our salvation—our born-again experience. While this role is absolutely pivotal in granting us entry into the Kingdom of God, we must be mindful of His other functions so that we can relate to Him successfully while living as citizens *of* the Kingdom.

## WHO IS THE HOLY SPIRIT?

*Empowerer.* This term is just as valid as "Counselor," "Comforter," "Helper," or "Advocate"—all translations of the one Greek word, *parakletos*. This word means the one called to your side to help in your time of need. Therefore, the name given depends upon the need. If a person was attempting to do that which is humanly impossible, the Empowerer would be needed.

*Evangelist.* The Holy Spirit is the great "Evangelist" of the church. He continues to use healings, signs, wonders, and His gifts to draw lost people to Jesus. Sadly, critics present a very truncated, limited understanding of the power and majesty of the Holy Spirit. God has not chosen to limit Himself, His sovereignty, or His ability to communicate to His people outside of the Bible. In His majesty glory, God continues to

> *The Holy Spirit shows us in the Bible what our inheritance is.*

create faith by His word, but this word is not limited to the Bible. He still comes to people and calls them to obedience in specific ways that are not possible if limited to the Bible. Again, these supernatural calls will never contradict what is already written; only bring the essence of Scripture into a personal relevance for us and our situations

*The Illuminator.* The Holy Spirit is the Illuminator of Scripture. He uses Scripture to convict us of sin and to make us aware of His will and ways in many things. He applies scriptural passages to our lives. He causes us to hunger for His presence and power so that we might bring glory to Jesus.

The Holy Spirit shows us in the Bible what our inheritance is. He led Luke to record His own activity in the book of Acts, and He laid out for all to see the various ways He led the early church, not just the apostles, but the deacons, evangelists, and other lay persons. The Scriptures teach us to desire not only the fruit of the Spirit but His gifts as well.

## QUESTIONS ABOUT THE HOLY SPIRIT

*Is speaking in tongues essential to be filled with the Holy Spirit?* It is important to realize there are many in the Charismatic Movement who do not believe one must speak in tongues in order to be filled with the Spirit. While tongues is certainly a gift and blessing it is not mandatory for an individual to be filled with the Spirit, nor is it the sure sign of the baptism of the Spirit.

*Does the Holy Spirit move in unusual ways—like causing people to fall down?* We note that the disciples were accused of "acting drunk" on the day of Pentecost. Also, it is not biblically or historically accurate to say that the phenomena of falling under the Spirit's power, being overwhelmed by the Spirit, or being "slain in the Spirit" is absent from Scripture.

In Daniel 10:7-11 it states,

> *I, Daniel, was the only one who saw the vision; the men with me did not see it, but such terror overwhelmed them that they fled and hid themselves. So I was left alone, gazing at this great vision; I had no strength left, my face turned deathly pale and I was helpless. Then I heard Him speaking, and as I listened to Him, I fell into a deep sleep, my face to the ground.*
>
> *A hand touched me and set me trembling on my hands and knees. He said, "Daniel, you who are highly esteemed, consider carefully the words I am about to speak to you, and stand up, for I have now been sent to you." And when He said this to me, I stood up trembling.*

*What are the keys to operating in God's power?* We cannot overlook the nature of faith as hearing and obeying the *rhema* words of God. If God does not communicate in this manner as is portrayed in both the Old and New Testaments, then the primary understanding of the meaning of faith has been made impossible for modern-day disciples to duplicate. The primary biblical meaning of faith is contingent upon receiving communications from God that are to be obeyed.

Thus, the key to operating in the supernatural power of the Spirit is faith, which is demonstrated through obedience. Even though we have examples of people who have been healed or experienced a miracle apart from expressed faith, by and large faith is the common denominator to receiving from God.

*What about the "laying on of hands"?* In Hebrews 6:1-2, we read about the doctrine of the "laying on of hands" and how it is considered an elementary matter of the faith. What does the doctrine of the laying on of hands represent? It represents the grace of God to do any of the following: bless, heal, or impart a gift.[106]

I am the first to admit that it is not the person laying on hands who causes the activation of a grace gift; it is the Sovereign Lord of the church who is the bestower of the gift via the Holy Spirit. Yet, it happens under the influence and at the instigation of the Spirit, often accompanied by "seeing what the Father/ Son/Spirit is doing," and sometimes with prophecy. When this scriptural passage is connected to the commissioning passages of Jesus and the Great Commission passage of Matthew 28, it becomes apparent that we need to see sanctification, discipleship, and honor for the Word as dependent upon reception of the Holy Spirit and His gifts.

> *The key to operating in the supernatural power of the Spirit is faith, which is demonstrated through obedience.*

## WHEN AM I FILLED WITH THE SPIRIT?

I want to give you some practical, biblical instruction on this controversial topic. If you have not yet experienced the wonderful baptism of the Spirit in your life, I pray that the following pages would prepare your heart to receive this powerfully infilling. If you have experienced the baptism of the Spirit, my prayer is that you would recognize that *there is more*. This does not mean that there is an upgraded Holy Spirit for you to receive, but rather that there is more of the Spirit's power dwelling inside of you that you can draw from, experience, and release to the world.

The normative biblical pattern is for the baptism or filling of the Spirit to follow conversion. The exception is for the baptism or filling with the Spirit to occur at conversion, which is not normative.

*More than one baptism.* Upon closer examination, the Bible speaks of more than one baptism. The Hebrews 6:2 text—*"instruction about baptisms"*—indicates the early apostolic and biblical instruction was about plural baptisms. First Corinthians 12:13 is in reference to conversion, or being baptized into the body of Christ. However, there is also water baptism, and there is being baptized in/with the Holy Spirit, which is not the same as water baptism or conversion, as indicated by Acts 8:16. This passage states, *"Because the Holy Spirit had not yet come upon any of them; they had simply been baptized into the name of the Lord Jesus."* These words are in reference to water baptism connected to the 1 Corinthians 12:13 experience. This text indicates it was possible to believe in the gospel, receive Christ, and be baptized without having necessarily received the baptism or filling with the Holy Spirit.

Peter's account of what happened in Acts 10, how Cornelius was saved, indicates that the Spirit can come upon and fill a person at the moment of conversion. In this case, it is without appearance of repentance, confession of Christ, or baptism prior to the Spirit coming upon the individual. This is definitely the exception to the more normative pattern of conversion. It is also the exception to the more normative experience of being filled or baptized with the Holy Spirit when He comes upon the person.

Again, the Acts 19:1-6 experience of being filled with the Spirit subsequent to the moment of salvation is more normative. These disciples were more likely the disciples of John the Baptist than disciples of Jesus. Paul's baptizing them in the name of Jesus at a time when they had not even heard of the Holy Spirit indicates this. When studying the teachings of the early church, it is evident that the Holy Spirit has a key emphasis in the preaching of the gospel, as indicated in Peter's Pentecost sermon. The term *disciple* was used of John the Baptist's disciples as well as disciples of Jesus.

Finally, one may ask about the question Paul asked the disciples, *"Did you receive the Holy Spirit when you first believed?"* (Acts 19:2). Does this not mean that they were expected to receive the Holy Spirit at conversion? I think the answer is yes and no.

## RECEIVING THE HOLY SPIRIT

There were two meanings for receiving the Holy Spirit. One deals with the indwelling and sealing aspect in the believers at conversion, while the other deals with receiving the Spirit, which came upon the disciples after conversion.

The first receiving is the baptism of 1 Corinthians 12:13. It is necessary for the experiential question of Paul in Galatians 3:2 to make rational sense: *"I would like to learn just one thing from you: Did you receive the Spirit by observing the law, or by believing what you heard?"* This question only makes sense if it were possible to know by experience when you received the Spirit, which, in this context, is referring to when they became Christians.

The Scripture also uses the term *"receive the Spirit"* for a subsequent (normative), or even simultaneous (outlier), conversion that is more than the Spirit indwelling, sealing, regenerating, and converting; it is the Spirit coming upon a person with power for greater consecration, holiness of lifestyle, and power for witness and miracles.[107]

When Paul received his filling with the Spirit in relation to his forgiveness of sins cannot be certain. It is clear that he was healed first, and then he told of being baptized for the forgiveness of sins. When exactly Ananias laid his hands upon him to be filled with the Spirit is not in the text, leaving us to conjecture.

It is clear that Cornelius and his household were filled with the Spirit as Peter begun to speak in Acts 10:44, 47; 11:15. It is significant that the Spirit "came upon" all who heard the message. Acts 10:43 notes the Spirit fell at the point in the message where Peter had just said, *"That everyone who believes in Him receives forgiveness of sins through His name."* There was evidence they had received the Spirit in 10:46: *"For they heard them speaking in tongues and praising God."*

## THE PATTERN FOR RECEIVING SPIRIT BAPTISM

I want to return to the discussion of Acts 19 and Paul's question, "Did you receive the Holy Spirit when you believed?" Versions translated before 1901 say, "Have you received the Holy Spirit *since* you believed?" Almost all translations after 1901 translate the passage as "Did you receive the Holy Spirit *when* you believed?" The NIV makes a note in the margin "or *after.*"[108]

Years ago I became curious about when this shift occurred. Suspecting that prejudice against the Pentecostal doctrine of subsequence (receiving the Spirit's baptism after conversion) may have been an influence, I contacted The Southern Baptist Theological Seminary in Louisville, Kentucky, and I asked the librarian to send me every English translation of Acts 19:1-6 prior to 1901. They all translated the passage, "Have you received the Holy Spirit *since* you believed?" After 1901 they all translated the passage as, "Did you receive the Holy Spirit *when* you believed?"

The earliest liturgy that has been discovered, *The Apostolic Traditions*, makes it clear the early church had a doctrine of sub-sequence in relation to the Spirit coming upon the newly baptized believers. Hands were placed upon them after their confession was made in water baptism. There were prayers for deliverance followed by prayers for the baptism with the Holy Spirit. This was seen as a sealing with the Spirit, not as confirmation.

The salvation experience was not complete without the sealing through the laying on of hands when the Spirit came upon the newly baptized. These were seen as two aspects of the one full experience of believing and being added to the church. It is in this double sense that the 1 Corinthians 12:13 passage is to be understood.[109]

I believe that the biblical text, *The Apostolic Traditions*, and present experiences do not support the position of cessationism, which is that one receives Holy Spirit baptism at the moment of conversion. Does this happen always? *No.* Does it happen sometimes? *Yes!* However, I do believe that every believer has the Holy Spirit living inside of him or her at the moment of conversion. The subsequent Spirit coming upon them empowers them and provides a sanctifying experience.

There is a difference between being put into Jesus by the Spirit (see 1 Cor. 12:13) and Jesus baptizing us with the Holy Spirit. *The Apostolic Traditions* link these two separate works of the Spirit into the baptism-initiation process of the early church that should occur within an extremely brief period of time.

# EMPOWERED FOR THE SAKE OF OTHERS

The first baptism is for us, for our salvation; the second type of baptism is for others who will be impacted by the power of the Spirit upon us. The baptism with the Holy Spirit is not self-centered, nor is the focus on the gifts of the Spirit self-centered. Rather, the focus of both the baptism and the gifts is to be empowered, to bring God's tangible mercy and power to the felt needs of other people.

They are other-focused and the ministry involving them is costly to the persons who serve others with the grace gifts. This ministry to others is part of the cross we are called to carry in Luke 9:23: *"Then He said to them all: 'If anyone would come after Me, he must deny himself and take up his cross daily and follow Me.'"* In fact, the expression of a lifestyle followed by signs, wonders, and demonstrations of the Spirit's

> *The first baptism is for us, for our salvation; the second type of baptism is for others who will be impacted by the power of the Spirit upon us.*

power is a practical demonstration of holiness. Holiness is not mere adherence to a moral code. A heart completely yielded to the commands of Christ evidences true holiness.

This is expressed by delivering those oppressed by the devil, healing the sick, and caring for widows, orphans, the poor, and sex victims. I agree it is important to be concerned for moral purity and the need to become Christlike in moral character. However, to be like Christ and to obey His commands is strongly emphasized in the upper room discourse in John 14–17 and in the Great Commission. It cannot stop at moral and ethical commands.

# A Call to Radical Discipleship

The call to discipleship is a summons to do what Jesus did. It is a call to do what He told us to do. It is a call to do what He died to make possible for us to do by His being *lifted up* on the cross, in the resurrection and in the ascension. This *lifting up* made possible the New Covenant in the Spirit, it made possible for us to be filled with the Holy Spirit, and it made possible our new birth. Him being lifted up made grace and grace gifts possible. From that place of being lifted up, He now pours out grace—not just undeserved mercy and forgiveness, but undeserved power in the Holy Spirit.

> *The call to discipleship is a summons to do what Jesus did.*

This theme is powerfully portrayed in John 14:8-21, in Jesus's interaction with Philip:

> *Philip said, "Lord, show us the Father and that will be enough for us."*
>
> *Jesus answered: "Don't you know Me, Philip, even after I have been among you such a long time? Anyone who has seen Me has seen the Father. How can you say, 'Show us the Father'? Don't you believe that I am in the Father, and that the Father is in Me? The words I say to you are not just My own. Rather, it is the Father, living in Me, who is doing His work. Believe Me when I say that I am in the Father and the Father is in Me; or at least believe on the evidence of the miracles themselves. I tell you the truth, anyone who has faith in Me will do what I have been doing. He will do even greater things than these, because I am going to the Father. And I will do whatever you ask in My name, so*

*that the Son may bring glory to the Father. You may ask Me for anything in My name, and I will do it.*

*"If you love Me, you will obey what I command. And I will ask the Father, and He will give you another Counselor to be with you forever—the Spirit of truth. The world cannot accept Him, because it neither sees Him nor knows Him. But you know Him, for He lives with you and will be in you. I will not leave you as orphans; I will come to you. Before long, the world will not see Me anymore, but you will see Me. Because I live, you also will live. On that day you will realize that I am in My Father, and you are in Me, and I am in you. Whoever has My commands and obeys them, he is the one who loves Me. He who loves Me will be loved by My Father, and I too will love him and show Myself to him."*

This passage gets to the heart of the matter. There is a close connection between loving Jesus and obeying Him. Obedience leads to intimate revelation from Him.

> *Obedience leads to intimate revelation from Him.*

The purpose of the power is to bring glory to the Father. It is important to note that in the larger context of John 14–17, the Father and the Son receive glory through what we do. It is important to see holiness as a doing, not just a being.

## JESUS: THE PERFECT EXAMPLE OF THE SPIRIT-FILLED LIFE

As a prototype for the Spirit-filled life, it helps us to understand how to interpret what Jesus said in John 20:21, *"As the Father has sent Me, I am sending you."* The prototype is the original, used as a model. If Jesus is our model, then we must see that our obedience, our discipleship unto Him, and our lives are to be like His. This is possible because of the Holy Spirit, because He is in us and we are in Him (see John 14:10; 17:21). Therefore, discipleship must produce disciples who look like the prototype—*Jesus*. This includes the areas of healing, deliverance, prophecy, and showing other acts of kindness and forgiveness.

Jesus was not so much a moral philosopher—He was much more the announcer of the power of the Kingdom of God, a healer, a deliverer, and a demonstrator of what can be done through the power of this Kingdom. The same Holy Spirit who empowered Jesus to do the works that He performed, likewise empowers believers today to accomplish the same works. Jesus and the first disciples did not receive an advantage over the contemporary church. They did not enjoy access to *another* Spirit. In fact, Paul tells us that the same power that was responsible for raising Christ from the dead, the Holy Spirit, lives inside each of us (see Rom. 8:11). This leaves us without excuse and serves as our summons into a life of supernatural discipleship.

> *If Jesus is our model, then we must see that our obedience, our discipleship unto Him, and our lives are to be like His.*

Sanctification, in its holistic sense, is following the example of Jesus Christ in every way. We cannot neglect the consecration, the commitment, and the commands dealing with advancing the Kingdom of God—such as healing the sick, delivering the oppressed, and healing the brokenhearted.

## COMMISSIONED TO FULLY PROCLAIM THE GOSPEL

Jesus, the prototype, was more than a Buddha and more than a moral religious philosopher. He was a deliverer from evil; evil that went beyond deception to include disease and demons. He was a deliverer from damnation. As our prototype, we should obey the commands He gave His disciples, and near the top of that list is to heal the sick and cast out demons.

In Matthew 10:7-8 it says, *"As you go, preach this message: 'The kingdom of heaven is near.' Heal the sick, raise the dead, cleanse those who have leprosy, drive out demons. Freely you have received, freely give."* We see a similar command to the seventy-two sent out in Luke 10:1, which reads, *"After this the Lord appointed seventy-two others and sent them two by two ahead of Him to every town and place where He was about to go."* The commission continues in Luke 10:9, *"Heal the sick who are there and tell them, 'The kingdom of God is near you.'"*

> *The same Holy Spirit who empowered Jesus to do the works that He performed, likewise empowers believers today to accomplish the same works.*

These commissionings are exemplary for the correct understanding of the Great Commissioning in Matthew 28:18-20,

> *All authority in heaven and on earth has been given to Me.*
> *Therefore go and make disciples of all nations, baptizing*
> *them in the name of the Father and of the Son and of the*
> *Holy Spirit, and teaching them to obey everything I have*
> *commanded you. And surely I am with you always, to the*
> *very end of the age.*

Sanctification that allows the disciple *not* to obey commands to heal the sick, cast out demons, cleanse the lepers, and raise the dead is an understanding of sanctification that lowers the bar for obedience and faith.

In Romans 15:17-19, Paul described what it means to fully proclaim the gospel: *"Therefore I glory in Christ Jesus in my service to*

*God. I will not venture to speak of anything except what Christ has accomplished through me in leading the Gentiles to obey God by what I have said and done—by the power of signs and miracles, through the power of the Spirit. So from Jerusalem all the way around to Illyricum, I have fully proclaimed the gospel of Christ."*

Critics would note that this verse cannot be seen as a basis for what it means to fully proclaim the gospel for our day, not because of sound biblical hermeneutics, but because of the cessationist hermeneutic to which they are wed.

The cessationist understanding calls into question the sufficiency of the Scriptures to reveal the biblical means of advancing the gospel, planting churches, and evangelizing the lost. A new non-biblical model, cessationism, is substituted for the biblical model, continuationism. The gospel itself is replaced with a new understanding that is foreign to its original intent. *Fully proclaiming* the gospel was presented in the context of *the power of signs and miracles.*

The cessationist perspective of the gospel is like selling term insurance—in order to get the benefit you have to die. The continuationist perspective of the gospel is like selling whole life insurance—you do not have to die to get the benefit, but you can rather enjoy benefits in this life.

It was the cessationist perspective of the gospel that caused Karl Marx to perceive Christianity as preaching "pie in the sky." He believed that the gospel, as it was preached in Europe, had little value to life in the present age because the preaching was focused on heaven, not earth.

The true evangelical gospel is neither a social gospel nor a personal gospel. It is also not only focused on going to heaven. The biblical gospel embraces both a social and a personal ethical dynamic with benefits for the present and future life. Our choices should not be an either/or option; instead, they should be a both/ and option. Pentecostal and Charismatic churches represent some of the best examples of a biblical gospel in action and expression.

## AUTHENTIC OR FALSE?

Some thought Jesus was the Messiah, the Prophet, or the Savior; others thought he was a madman, a blasphemer, doing what He did by the power of Beelzebub, not the Spirit of God. The vital question addressed by the controversy between cessationists and continuationists is whether or not words of knowledge related to healings, the healings themselves, the dead being raised, prophecies, the gift of tongues and interpretation of tongues, the signs, wonders, and miracles were from the Holy Spirit, the demonic realm, or from the flesh.

Truly, this is a valid question.

First, I do not believe that the flesh or the demonic realm has the power to raise the dead. Neither do I believe the demonic realm or the flesh can effect major healings that bring glory to the name of Jesus Christ. The flesh is incapable of conjuring up such a supernatural demonstration, and the demonic would not dare give glory to Jesus, as a kingdom divided against itself cannot stand (see Matt. 12:25-26).

Second, I believe that the Bible and experience addresses the reality of the power of the Holy Spirit being greater than the power of the enemy, the demonic, and infinitely more powerful than the ability of the human mind over matter or the human spirit.

Third, when it comes to minor healings, to alleged prophecies, and, yes, even to tongues and interpretation of tongues, I believe it becomes more difficult to discern the source because the kingdom of darkness and the power of the mind are realities. Darkness can counterfeit to a point, and the human mind is capable of manufacturing certain phenomena. However, these realities are of significantly less power than the power of the Holy Spirit.

It is true that speaking in tongues occurs in non-Christians, but the interpretation would be easier to discern because the message should be addressed to God. A message that would be inappropriate or theologically wrong would be easy to discern as not from God. In a more rare tongue that would be interpreted as a prophecy from God to people would need to meet both the theological test and the moral test. If the message contradicts the incarnation of the Son of God, is disparaging toward the historical Jesus, or violates the moral nature of the Triune God, then it would not be from God.

I invite you to be a Berean (see Acts 17:11) and consider the following biblical arguments for the continuation of healing, miracles, prophecy, tongues, and interpretation of tongues.

## THE CONTINUATION OF THE HOLY SPIRIT'S GIFTS

In this subsection, I will examine the biblical basis for the continuation of the gifts of the Spirit, including healing and working of miracles, throughout the history of the church. The Bible teaches that the gifts are to continue until Jesus returns. Furthermore, it is not expected that they would end with the death of the apostles or with the completion of the Bible.

God's gifts are irrevocable. Romans 11:29 is an obvious passage that explicitly rejects the teaching that spiritual gifts were only temporary and were to end 1) with the death of the apostles, 2) with the death of their immediate disciples, or 3) with the canonization of the Bible.[110]

Cessationists have argued that this passage has been taken out of context and does not apply to the gifts of the Spirit because it deals with Israel's election, not spiritual gifts. This is a tired argument because cessationists have the logic of the passage backward: it is not "the salvation of the Jews," to which this principle of continuation is limited. Rather, Paul appeals to a separate *universal principle*, the charismata and the calling of God are not withdrawn to show that *a specific case*, the salvation of the Jews, is assured. Ruthven argues that Romans 11:29 is a paraphrase of Isaiah 59:21, and given the context of the Isaiah passage, it is very similar to how it is used in the context of the "calling" of Jews in Acts 2:38-39.[111]

This verse actually teaches the opposite of cessationism, and it clearly teaches that God's gifts are irrevocable. Another translation, the King James Version, says they are *"without repentance,"* meaning God does not change His mind about giving them, ultimately taking them back.

### Dispensational Cessationism

Other Old Testament Scriptures also refute dispensational cessationism, which teaches that God only worked miracles during certain periods or dispensations. These periods were during times when God gave revelation about new doctrinal understanding. The truth is that miracles and healings occurred when it was not a so-called time of revelation.

There are also New Testament Scriptures that refute dispensational cessationism.[112] Much of the debate is centered around 1 Corinthians 13:8-10, which states, *"Love never fails. But where there are prophecies, they will cease; where there are tongues, they will be stilled; where there is knowledge, it will pass away. For we know in part and we prophesy in part, but when perfection comes, the imperfect disappears."*

The *perfect* is considered by cessationists to be the Bible; continuationists consider it as the second coming of Jesus. The second coming of Jesus was the interpretation given by orthodox Catholic patristic fathers. This verse was actually used to confront Montanists in the second century.[113]

Galatians 3:5 states, *"Does God give you His Spirit and work miracles among you because you observe the law, or because you believe what you heard?"* The verb tense is present, not past, and would imply that the miraculous nature of the life of the church continued even when their apostle was not present among them.

Also, in Ephesians 1:13-23, Paul distinguishes between the faith with which they have believed and were saved (1:13), the faith with which they continue in the Lord (1:15), and the further operation of the Spirit in his prayers for them (1:17-23). These constant prayers are for God to *"give you the Spirit of wisdom and revelation, so that you may know Him better"* (Eph. 1:17).

Receiving the Holy Spirit continues until the redemption of those who are God's possession, until the second coming of Christ. The giving of the Spirit is extremely powerful. When a person understands that glory and power are synonyms, and that the primary way God receives glory in the Bible is through signs and wonders, miracles and healings, it implies that all the gifts have to continue until Jesus returns.[114] Healings, miracles, signs and wonders were the number one way God received glory in Scripture.[115]

Ephesians urges believers to *"be strong in the Lord and in His mighty power"* (Eph. 6:10). They are to put on the full armor of God and pray in the Spirit on all occasions with various prayers and requests. The way to be *"strong in the Lord and in His mighty power"* is by putting on *"the whole armor of God"* and by *"pray-ing in the Spirit."* Many commentators even believe *"praying in the Spirit"* may be a reference to praying in tongues. His mighty power surely includes the power to heal and the working of miracles.

Another way of looking at the connection between fruit and glory is to understand that glory equals power, and fruit, as used by Paul here, can also mean the fruit of John 15, which reveals the inner working of the Spirit that makes believers fruitful in doing the powerful work of Jesus. This working of the Spirit begins with love, which is a fruit of the Spirit, and appears to open up more knowledge and depth of insight (see Phil. 1:9-10). This knowledge and insight is revelatory and reveals the purpose of God, enabling a person to be confident in his or her prayers, making them more powerful to manifest miracles and healings.

The "fruit of righteousness" means moral fruit and supernat-ural deeds, especially miracles and healings. These all come by the Spirit of God. The intimacy, the abounding in insight and depth of knowledge, does not refer to insight or depth of knowl-edge of doctrine or theology, but rather of God Himself, and of God's directives for what He wants to do in the immediate pres-ent or upcoming ministry opportunity. As believers learn His ways, and learn how to hear His communications, these revela-tions become the source of their faith to do or produce the "fruits of righteousness."[116]

Peter also indicates the gifts will continue. God's power is meant to shield believers until the salvation that is consummated in the end of time (see 1 Pet. 4:7-12). Peter is anticipating the end of time coming soon. In verse 10 he admonishes, *"Each one should use whatever gift he has received to serve others, faithfully administering God's grace in its various forms."* A gift is a form of God's grace.

THE ESSENTIAL GUIDE TO THE POWER OF THE HOLY SPIRIT

The various gifts reflect various forms of grace. In this light, to say that some of the gifts ended would be tantamount to saying some of God's grace ended. There is nothing in the text that hints that these forms of God's grace were to end before the end of time.[117]

Paul, Peter, and John have an understanding of the gifts continuing until Jesus returns. In 1 John 2:26-28, John refers to an anointing from God that is to remain in believers.[118] This "anointing is real and not counterfeit." He encourages the believers to continue in Jesus so they will be confident and unashamed before Him at His coming. This is referring to Jesus's second coming. There is no indication in this text and its context that a time would arise when the believers would no longer need this anointing or it would be taken away from them.

> **We need the power of the Holy Spirit; it is nonnegotiable.**

Thus, the Spirit's power is available for you today just as it was available to the early church.

## YOUR GREAT COMMISSION

Paul wrote to the Corinthians,

> *When I came to you, brothers, I did not come with eloquence or superior wisdom as I proclaimed to you the testimony about God. For I resolved to know nothing while I was with you except Jesus Christ and Him crucified. I came to you in weakness and fear, and with much trembling. My message and my preaching were not with wise and persuasive words, but with a demonstration of the Spirit's power, so that your faith might not rest on men's wisdom, but on God's power.* (1 Corinthians 2:1-5)

We need the power of the Holy Spirit; it is nonnegotiable. It is not an evangelical side-item. It should *not* be a topic of theological debate. Paul expressly states that it was not rhetoric and words alone that brought his listeners to faith in Christ. Rather, he presents the true source of his evangelistic effectiveness as a demonstration of the Spirit's power in his midst.

When preaching the gospel to Animists, Muslims, Hindus, Buddhists, or New Agers, whether in our present time or throughout the unfolding history of the church, it is not the preaching alone that convicts or convinces the people that what is said is true. More accurately, preaching the Bible is not what convinces those from non-Christian

> *It is not simply what is said that causes people to turn to Christ. It is what is said and done.*

cultures—especially cultures with other major religions—that what is preached is the truth. Saying, "the Bible says" does not actually bring authority to what is being said. Like the apostle Paul, St. Patrick, and the Bakers in Mozambique today, it is not simply what is said that causes people to turn to Christ. It is what is said *and* done.

Contemporary missionaries have communicated their inability to win Muslims to the Lord using reason, arguments, and persuasion alone; it was through the Muslims seeing miracles, signs and wonders, healings, deliverances, dreams, and visions of Jesus—in essence, experiencing something supernatural—that caused them to believe in the gospel, in Jesus Christ, and then in the Scriptures. Power seems to work cooperatively with Scripture, being a source of validation that what is being heralded as truth is actually *the truth*.

This is why we are in desperate need of the Spirit's power in our lives today. If we want to walk in the fruitfulness of the early church, we need not look for a new strategy or even cry for a new outpouring to come out of heaven. We are not seeking something new; we are seeking something profoundly biblical and modeled in the life of Jesus, in the culture of the New Testament church, and in the lives of believers throughout the centuries.

In order to move forward, we must go back to Pentecost. Again, this is not to suggest that we need another Pentecostal outpouring from heaven, but we certainly need one to emerge from the lives of men and women who recognize that the Spirit of the living God energizes and empowers them to follow Jesus's model, in both attitude and action, in both word and in demonstration. We need to cease upholding the fruit of the Spirit to the neglect of the gifts of the Spirit, and, likewise, emphasizing the character of Christ while considering His power, signs, and wonders as secondary. Remember, it is not an either/or decision.

> *We are not seeking something new; we are seeking something profoundly biblical and modeled in the life of Jesus, in the culture of the New Testament church, and in the lives of believers throughout the centuries.*

The Great Commission indicates that people who become Christians are supposed to be taught to do what Jesus taught the disciples to do. Healing the sick and casting out demons is what Jesus taught them to do. There is no indication that these things were meant to continue only until the Bible was canonized. As long as there is a baptism in the name of the Father, the Son, and the Holy Spirit, the newly baptized are to be taught to heal the sick and cast out demons. This includes you!

Dr. Ruthven believes that the Great Commission and the commissioning of the twelve and the seventy-two were indicative of Jesus's desire for His followers throughout all generations to obey the commissioning. The commissioning of the twelve and of the seventy-two is the pattern and substance for the Great Commission, and represents your commission today.[119]

When you received the Holy Spirit, you received the power of the Kingdom of heaven. It is time for us to fully believe that what we received in the Holy Spirit is supernatural, and thus, completely sufficient to fulfill the Great Commission that Jesus mandated in Matthew 28 and Mark 16.

I want to take this moment to pray for you to experience everything that you just read about. As you read these words, I ask you to receive what they are praying over you. Personalize them and access every wonderful gift that the Father has waiting for you in the Holy Spirit!

> *"Father, in the name of Jesus I ask that You would meet the faith and hunger of the person holding this book. I bless this person in the name of Jesus and ask for Your Holy Spirit's fire to come upon him or her. I ask that You would release Your compassion and love into this person's heart right now. I ask that You would especially impart the gifts of word of knowledge, healing, prophecy, and the workings of miracles through this person in the days ahead. As he or she waits in Your presence, Father, with hands outstretched and palms raised, I ask that Your power would touch these hands. Multiply Your power. Increase Your power. Baptize this reader in Your Holy Spirit, and fill this soul with the peace of the Prince of peace. In Jesus' name, Amen".*

*This prayer also appears in Randy Clark's *There is More! The Secret to Experiencing God's Power to Change Your Life* (Grand Rapids, MI: Chosen Books, 2013), 226.

# THE FRUIT OF DIVINE ENCOUNTERS

What kind of fruit does a divine encounter produce? I am referring to encounters of the following kind: receiving an impartation (i.e., a transference of the anointing or gifting), dreams, angelic visitation, deliverance, prophetic declaration, or a visitation from the Lord. Conversion was not included because the subjects were already saved when they had these other encounters; of course, conversion is the most important, foundational divine encounter, but usually these encounters occurred post-conversion.[120]

The Executive Director of Global Awakening, Dr. Tom Jones, did doctoral research that reviewed the fruit of manifestations upon relationships and the fruit of manifestations upon the fruit of the Spirit, as well as the fruit of the work of ministry and moving in the gifts. In Appendix A, I have placed Dr. Jones's charts and figures taken from his thesis. I highly recommend anyone who wants a fair and scientific study of the effects of divine encounters, using quantitative and qualitative methods of analysis, to read his thesis.[121] Here you will be able to review Dr. Jones's analysis of his study with the results of his survey of over 130 pastors and itinerant ministers. The evidence strongly points to the significant fruit in every area studied.

Appendix B provides the link to several videos that record miraculous healing testimonies, including one testimony of Susan Starr, who was in hospice facing death without any medical basis for hope of recovery.

In Appendix C, I have included the charts that depict the results of my doctoral thesis on the verification of healings of people with chronic pain or range of mobility restrictions due to surgery involving implanted materials.

# APPENDIX A

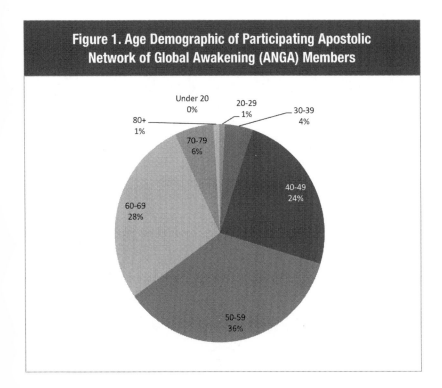

**Figure 1. Age Demographic of Participating Apostolic Network of Global Awakening (ANGA) Members**

Under 20 0%

20-29 1%

30-39 4%

80+ 1%

70-79 6%

40-49 24%

60-69 28%

50-59 36%

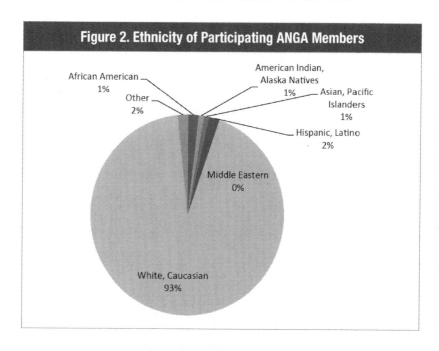

Figure 2. Ethnicity of Participating ANGA Members

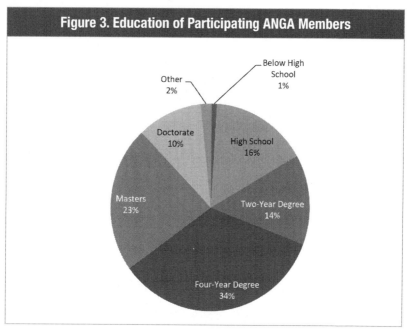

Figure 3. Education of Participating ANGA Members

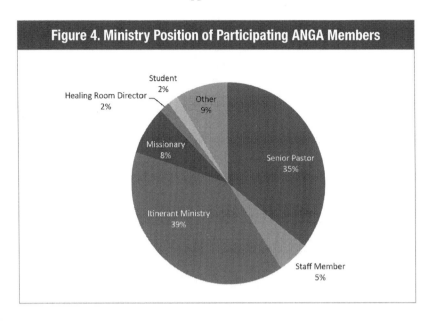

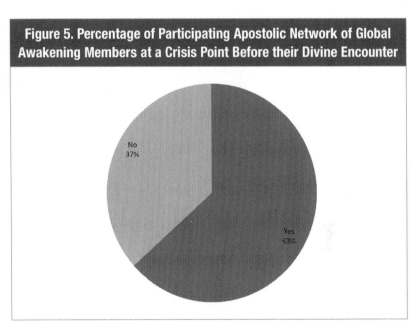

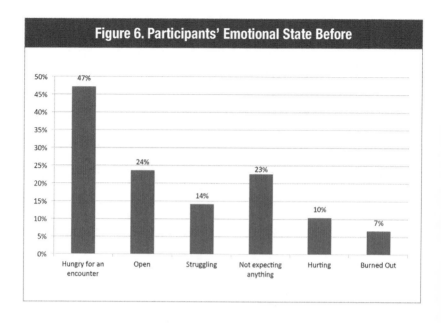

Figure 6. Participants' Emotional State Before

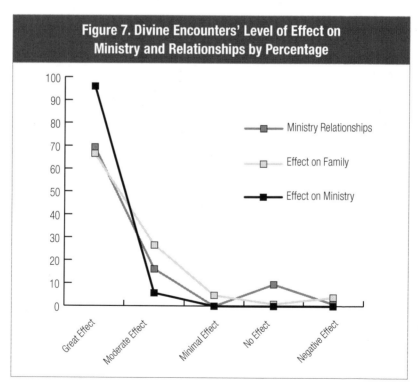

Figure 7. Divine Encounters' Level of Effect on Ministry and Relationships by Percentage

*Appendix A*

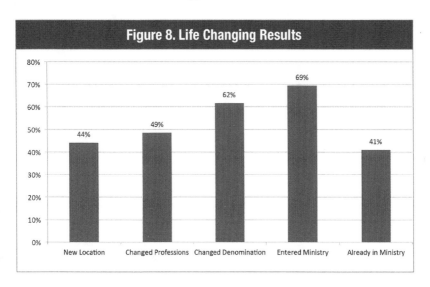

Figure 8. Life Changing Results

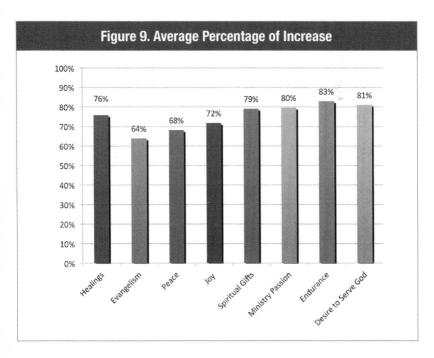

Figure 9. Average Percentage of Increase

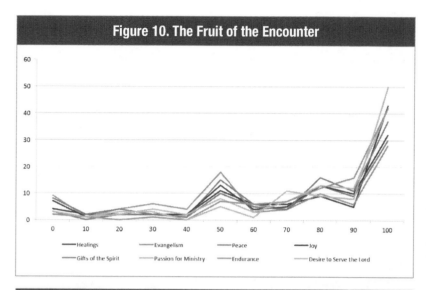

Figure 10. The Fruit of the Encounter

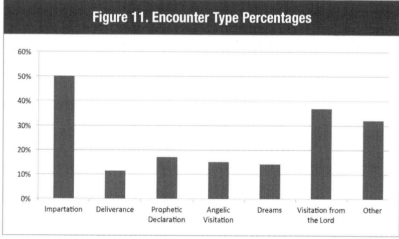

Figure 11. Encounter Type Percentages

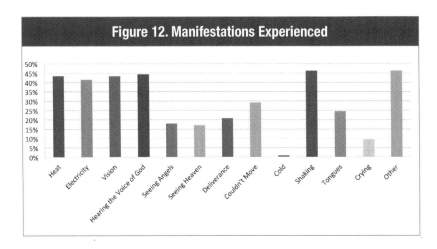

Figure 12. Manifestations Experienced

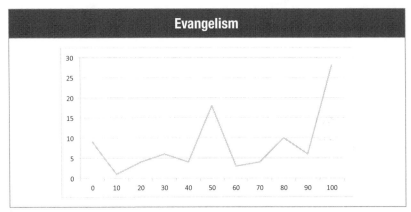

Evangelism

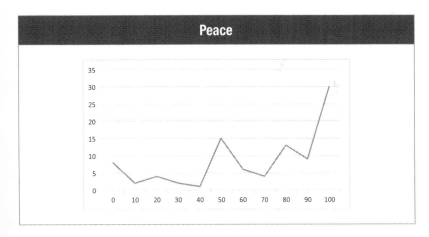

Peace

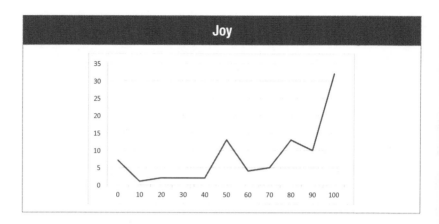

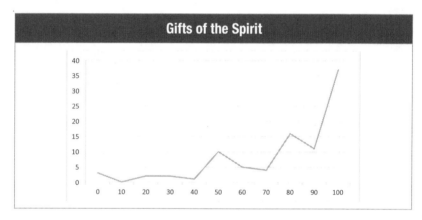

# Appendix A

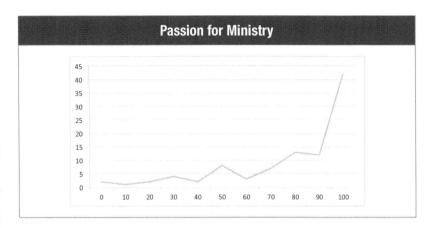

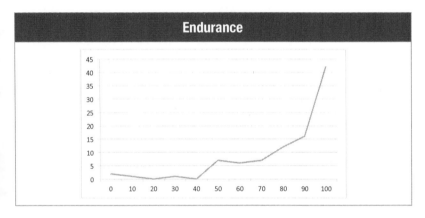

# APPENDIX B

Listed below are links to video testimonies of miraculous healings, specifically related to surgically implanted materials. These are based upon my doctoral research.

- First time I ever prayed for surgically implanted material: http://youtu.be/BYUGWOIB-R4
- Boy's foot healed: http://youtu.be/e4O7gZrWuwg
- Woman does what she previously could not do: http://youtu.be/9E0LTutJBVg
- Man can no longer feel metal plate in his arm: http://youtu.be/xv_xKe7Xwxs
- Essure testimony: http://youtu.be/BSSpTh8HzYA
- Girl with metal in wrist that disappears: http://youtu.be/Uni9tUTwTSM
- Wrestler who had metal in his toe: http://youtu.be/Yeuqeh6LyhM
- Man's back healed: http://www.youtube.com/watch?v=hSuA4K2GhU4&feature=youtu.be
- Susan Starr testimony: http://youtu.be/XpO_1cgws7Q

# APPENDIX C

Tables from my thesis, including the calculation of pain and range of mobility healings in persons with surgically implanted materials. The below tables are listed by continent.

| Table 1. 2012 Healing Percentages by Continent | | | | |
|---|---|---|---|---|
| Meetings in Asia/Australia | # of Persons with SIM | # of SIM Persons with Pain & ROM | # of Persons Healed | Healed (in %) |
| Churchlands Church, Australia | 4 | 2 | 1 | 53% |
| Churchlands Church, Australia | 4 | 2 | 2 | 100% |
| Kenmore Baptist Church, Australia | 28 | 13 | 4 | 30% |
| Dayspring Church, Australia | 4 | 2 | 2 | 100% |
| Revival Christian Church, Hong Kong | 8 | 4 | 2 | 53% |
| Revival Christian Church, Hong Kong | 6 | 3 | 2 | 71% |
| The Vine Church, Hong Kong | 2 | 1 | 2 | 100% |
| WLI Conference, Korea | 10 | 5 | 1 | 21% |
| Daegu Full Gospel, Korea | 5 | 2 | 2 | 85% |

| Daegu Full Gospel, Korea | 10 | 5 | 1 | 21% |
|---|---|---|---|---|
| **Total Asia/Australia** | **81** | **38** | **19** | |
| **Mean Asia/Australia** | **8** | **4** | **2** | **50%** |

| Meetings in Europe | # of Persons with SIM | # of SIM Persons with Pain & ROM | # of Persons Healed | Healed (in %) |
|---|---|---|---|---|
| Cultural Center, Denmark | 20 | 9 | 1 | 11% |
| Cultural Center, Denmark | 21 | 10 | 7 | 71% |
| Holy Trinity Swiss Cottage, England | 16 | 8 | 1 | 13% |
| Edinburgh, Scotland | 10 | 5 | 1 | 21% |
| Catch the Fire Conference, England | 32 | 15 | 7 | 47% |
| Catch the Fire Conference, England | 9 | 4 | 3 | 71% |
| Holy Trinity Brompton, England | 11 | 5 | 2 | 39% |
| **Total Europe** | **119** | **56** | **22** | |
| **Mean Europe** | **17** | **8** | **3** | **39%** |

| Meetings in North America | # of Persons with SIM | # of SIM Persons with Pain & ROM | # of Persons Healed | Healed (in %) |
|---|---|---|---|---|
| Master's Touch Intl. Church, Florida | 11 | 5 | 2 | 39% |
| Cross Roads Church, Illinois | 24 | 11 | 8 | 66% |
| Shekinah Glory Church, Tennessee | 6 | 3 | 1 | 35% |
| New Life City, New Mexico | 31 | 15 | 2 | 14% |
| Katie Souza Conference, Arizona | 20 | 9 | 5 | 50% |
| Heartland Assembly, Iowa | 14 | 7 | 2 | 30% |
| Elim Fellowship, New York | 33 | 21 | 8 | 38% |

*Appendix C*

| Church | # | # | # | % |
|---|---|---|---|---|
| Evangel Church, Kentucky | 33 | 13 | 2 | 15% |
| Urbana Vineyard Church, Illinois | 61 | 27 | 11 | 41% |
| Awakened to Destiny, Colorado | 83 | 34 | 9 | 26% |
| WLI Conference, California | 11 | 7 | 3 | 43% |
| Apostolic Resource Center, PA | 25 | 7 | 1 | 14% |
| East Gate Church, PA | 17 | 8 | 2 | 25% |
| Total North America | 369 | 167 | 56 | |
| Mean North America | 28 | 13 | 4 | 34% |

| Meetings in South America | # of Persons with SIM | # of SIM Persons with Pain & ROM | # of Persons Healed | Healed (in %) |
|---|---|---|---|---|
| Igreja Videira, Brazil | 12 | 8 | 4 | 51% |
| Igreja Videira, Brazil | 16 | 11 | 9 | 85% |
| Ministério Internacional, Brazil | 5 | 3 | 1 | 30% |
| Igreja Batista Evangélica, Brazil | 5 | 3 | 1 | 30% |
| Igreja Batista Nova Canaã, Brazil | 8 | 5 | 5 | 95% |
| Plentitude Igreja Em Células, Brazil | 21 | 13 | 4 | 31% |
| Logos Church, Brazil | 24 | 17 | 3 | 18% |
| Logos Church, Brazil | 13 | 8 | 1 | 13% |
| Communidade Cristã, Brazil | 40 | 17 | 2 | 12% |
| Communidade Cristã, Brazil | 36 | 28 | 9 | 32% |
| Shalom Communidade Cristã, Brazil | 19 | 18 | 9 | 50% |
| Igreja Batista Áqua Vida, Brazil | 27 | 14 | 4 | 29% |
| Total South America | 226 | 145 | 52 | |
| Mean South America | 19 | 12 | 4 | 36% |

# NOTES

1. Jon Ruthven, *On the Cessation of the Charismata: The Protestant Polemic on Post-Biblical Miracles* (Tulsa, OK: Word and Spirit Press, 2011); Jon Ruthven, *What's Wrong With Protestant Theology? Traditions vs. Biblical Emphasis* (Tulsa, OK: Word and Spirit Press, 2013); Gary Greig and Kevin Springer, eds., *The Kingdom and the Power: Are Healing and the Spiritual Gifts Used By Jesus and the Early Church Meant for the Church Today?* (Ventura, CA: Regal Books, 1993); Craig S. Keener, *Miracles: The Credibility of the New Testament Accounts*, 2 vols. (Grand Rapids, MI: Baker Academic, 2011).

2. Vinson Synan, *The Century of the Holy Spirit* (Nashville: Thomas Nelson, 2001), 166.

3. Ibid. Also see John Calvin, *Institutes of the Christian Religion*, John T. McNeil, ed., 4 vols. (Philadelphia: Westminster, 1960), 1:15-31; 4:1466-84. Also see Calvin's *New Testament Commentaries: 1 Corinthians* (Grand Rapids: Eerdmans, 1960), 258-73.

4. Thomas Boys, *The Suppressed Evidenced: Or Proofs of the Miraculous Faith and Experience of the Church of Jesus Christ In All Ages* (1832), http://books.google.com/books?id=JkopAAAAYAAJ&printsec=frontcover&source=gbs_ge_summary_r&cad=0#v=onepage&q&f=false (accessed March 5, 2012), 94-110.

5. Ibid., 162-67.

6. Ibid., 186-203.

7. Eddie L. Hyatt, *2000 Years of Charismatic Christianity* (Lake Mary, FL: Charisma House, 2002), 74.

8. Johannes Mathesius, *Luthers Leben in Predigten* (Prague, Czech Republic: Herausgegeben von G. Loesche, 1906), 399; quoted by John Horsch, "The Faith of the Swiss Brethren, II" *Mennonite Quarterly Review* 5, no. 1 (1931), 16.

9. Jeff Doles, *Miracles and Manifestations of the Holy Spirit in the History of the Church* (Seffner, FL: Walking Barefoot Ministries, 2008), 138-42. Doles is dependent upon Seckendorf's *History of Lutheranism*.

10. Randy Clark, *There Is More! The Secret to Experiencing God's Power to Change Your Life* (Bloomington, MN: Chosen Books, 2013).

11. Randy Clark and Bill Johnson, *The Essential Guide to Healing: Equipping All Christians to Pray for the Sick* (Bloomington, MN: Chosen Books, 2011).

12. I have chosen to capitalize Charismatics due to the fact that across the world there are denominations called Charismatic in the same way that in the United States Pentecostals have formed denominations.

13. Kenneth Hagin Sr., *The Midas Touch: A Balanced Approach to Biblical Prosperity* (Tulsa, OK: Rhema Bible Church, 2000).

14. Paul King, *Only Believe: Examining the Origin and Development of Classic and Contemporary "Word of Faith" Theologies* (Tulsa, Ok: Word and Spirit Press, 2009); Joe McIntyre, *E. W. Kenyon: and His Message of Faith the True Story* (Bothell, WA: Empowering Grace Ministries, 2010). McIntyre gained access to Kenyon's personal diaries that disproved the historical reconstruction by D. R. McConnell in his book, *A Different Gospel*. Both King and McIntyre prove the thesis of McConnell to be incorrect.

15. In 1995, I was so concerned for balance that I compiled a book called *Power, Holiness, and Evangelism*, believing that the church needed not an either/or option—power *or* holiness—but a both/and option if it was to be most successful in evangelism. Randy Clark, *Power, Holiness, and Evangelism: Rediscovering God's Purity, Power, and Passion for the Lost* (Shippensburg, PA: Destiny Image, 1999).

16. For clarification regarding these three models of evangelism, see Randy Clark, *Evangelism Unleashed: Reembracing the Catalyst of Power* (Mechanicsburg, PA: Global Awakening, 2005), esp. chapter 2. See also Randy Clark, "Global Impact of Healing on Evangelism and Missions, Part 1 & 2," in *School of Healing and Impartation: Revival Phenomena and Healing Workbook*, (Mechanicsburg, PA: Global Awakening, 2010).

*Notes*

17. Elizabeth A. Livingstone, *Studia Patristica,* Papers Presented to the Tenth International Conference on Patristic Studies (Leuven, Belgium: Peeters Press, 1989), 22:189.

18. Morton T. Kelsey, *Healing and Christianity* (New York, NY: Harper and Row, Publishers, 1976), 186-87.

19. Robin Mackintosh, *Augustine of Canterbury: Leadership, Spirituality, and Mission* (London: Canterbury Press, 2013), 149.

20. George Montague and Killian McDonnell, *Christian Initiation and Baptism in the Holy Spirit: Evidence from the First Eight Centuries* (Collegeville, MN: Liturgical, 1994), 108.

21. Russel Conwell, "Chapter 7: Wonderful Healing," in *Life of Charles Haddon Spurgeon: The World's Great Preacher* (Philadelphia, PA: Edgewood Publishing, 1892).

22. Jack Deere, *Surprised by the Voice of God: How God Speaks Today Through Prophecies, Dreams, and Visions* (Grand Rapids, MI: Zondervan Publishing House, 1998), 70-78.

23. Falling under the power refers to the contemporary and ancient experience of not being able to remain standing due to the power of God touching one's body. Pentecostals call it "slain in the Spirit," Catholics prefer to call it "resting in the Spirit," eighteenth-century Methodists called it "losing all strength," and nineteenth-century Methodists called it "swooning." This phenomenon occurred during most periods of revival throughout the history of the church. It can also be seen in the Bible.

For more insight into this and other phenomena of the Spirit, see Paul King, "Supernatural Physical Manifestations in the Evangelical and Holiness Revival Movements." The Pneuma Foundation: Resources for Spirit-Empowered Ministry. www.pneumafoundation.org/resources/articles/manifestations.pdf (accessed May 14, 2012); R. Edward Miller, *Cry for Me Argentina: Revival Begins in City Bell* (Brentwood, UK: Sharon, 1988); H. A. Baker, *Visions Beyond the Veil* (New Kensington, PA: Whitaker House, 2006); Vinson Synan, *The Holiness-Pentecostal Tradition: Charismatic Movements in the Twentieth Century* (Cambridge, UK: Eerdmans, 1997), 24-25; Peter Cartwright, *Autobiography of Peter Cartwright: The Backwoods Preacher,* ed. W. B. Strickland (Ann Arbor, MI: University of Michigan Library, 2005), 259; Charles Finney, *An Autobiography* (Westwood, NJ: Fleming H. Revell, 1908), 20-21; John Wesley, *The Journal of the Rev. John Wesley,* ed. Nehemiah Curnock

205

(London, UK: Epworth, 1911), 239-40; Arnold A. Dallimore, *George Whitefield: God's Anointed Servant in the Great Revival of the Eighteenth Century* (Wheaton, IL: Crossway, 1990), 52.

In one meeting in the Belgian Congo in 1914, C. T. Studd recorded, "The whole place was charged as if with an electrical current. Men were falling, jumping, laughing, crying, singing, confessing, and some shaking terribly. It was a terrible sight.... This particular one can best be described as a spiritual tornado. People were literally flung to the floor or over the forms, yet no one was hurt.... As I led in prayer, the Spirit came down in mighty power, sweeping the congregation. My whole body literally trembled with the power. We saw a marvellous [sic] sight, people literally filled and drunk with the Spirit" [Winkie Pratney, *Revival— Its Principles & Personalities: Twenty Centuries of Vision & Visitation* (Lafayette, LA: Huntington, 1994), 189-90].

See also Greig and Springer, *The Kingdom and the Power*, 133-74; Richard and Kathryn Riss, *Images of Revival: Another Wave Rolls In* (Shippensburg, PA: Revival Press, 1997), 17-48.

The reason for giving so much information in this footnote is the importance of realizing that there is a real power that comes to people during prayer in Christ's name, often making them fall to the ground, shake, or feel heat so intensely that they sweat, sometimes so much so that in an air-conditioned room, while no one else is sweating, their shirt becomes completely soaked in sweat, or sometimes the feeling is icy cold instead of heat. The cause of these manifestations must be considered key to the understanding of healing and miracles due to prayer in Jesus's name.

24.  Randy Clark and Gary Greig, "Response to Critics: A Response to the Critic Andrew Strom," Global Awakening (2013), http://andrewstromresponse.com (accessed December 19, 2013). Abraham hardly laughed just to release stress in this situation in Genesis 17:17, because it is immediately followed in 17:18 by his pleading with the Lord and the Lord correcting his misguided desire. Such abnormal laughter clearly came from the Lord manifesting His presence to Abraham and speaking His word to Abraham.

25.  Ibid. See also Georg Bertram, *Theological Dictionary of the New Testament*, ed. Gerhard Kittel and Gerhard Friedrich, trans. Geoffrey W. Bromiley (Grand Rapids, MI: Eerdmans, 1977), s.v. "Energeo," 2:652.

26. Ibid. The Spirit of the Lord is described as "rushing upon" Samson in Judges 14:6, 14:19, and 15:14; upon Saul so that he "prophesies" in 1 Samuel 10:6 and 10:10; and upon David when Samuel anointed him with oil in 1 Samuel 16:13. The interesting thing about the Hebrew verb *tsalakh*, "rush upon," is that it is not only used to describe the Holy Spirit being poured out on individuals, but it is also used of *fire* rushing upon Israel in Amos 5:6—*"Seek the Lord and live, lest He rush like fire upon the house of Joseph; it will consume, and Bethel will have no one to quench it."*

27. Ibid. Acts 6:15 says Stephen's face was *"like the face of an angel,"* to which passage compare Acts 12:7, Ezekiel 40:3, Daniel 10:6, Luke 2:9, and Matthew 28:2-3.

28. Ibid. We should not be surprised that God's Spirit moved among Jewish people who were not yet saved. The story in Acts 10:1-6 of Cornelius being visited by an angel of the Lord before he was saved shows that God is reaching out to pre-believers through His Spirit and His angels to bring them to Jesus. So the following examples of the Holy Spirit's power in early Judaism represent, in my opinion, God reaching out trying to bring Jewish people to their Messiah, Jesus (John 1:9 says of Jesus, *"[He is] the true light, who gives light to everyone, [who] was coming into the world"*). The presence and power of God's Spirit was marked in early Judaism by light and radiance, producing a radiant face. E. Sjöberg, in *Theological Dictionary of the New Testament*, 6:381-82.

29. Colossians 1:29: "To this end I labor, struggling with all His energy, which so powerfully works in me."

30. This was an American Pentecostal context statement, as I realize there are very devout Presbyterians around the world, particularly in Brazil, that do not drink any alcohol. Likewise, this statement is not meant to universally portray all Catholics, Lutherans, and Presbyterians as given to alcohol. This is hardly the case; unfortunately, it was the perception of many in the Pentecostal church during the initial emergent of the Charismatic Movement.

31 Ruthven, *On the Cessation of the Charismata*, 173.

32. Ibid., 173-74.

33. Ruthven, *What's Wrong with Protestant Theology?*, 299-300.

34. Joseph Bentivegna, "The Witness of St. Augustine on the Action of the Holy Spirit in the Church and the Praxis of Charismata in His Time," *Studia Patristica* 22 (1989), 198, citing Sermo 243, 6, 5.

35. Ibid., 199, citing De Civitate Dei 22, 8, 14; cf. Sermo 323, 2, 2.

36. Ruthven, *On the Cessation of the Charismata*, 195-219.

37. Ibid., 171.

38. Ibid., 203-219, esp. 208-212.

39. Ibid., 214. Ruthven is referencing G. W. H. Lampe, *A Patristic Greek Lexicon* (Oxford: Clarendon, 1961), 66; see also, Cyril, *Is.*3.2 (2.397E) and John of Damascus, *Hom.* 4:30 (MPG 96.632c).

40. Ibid., 216.

41. Ibid., 216-17.

42. Ibid., 216.

43. Ibid.

44. Ibid., 218.

45. Ibid., 218, original emphasis.

46. Ibid., 219.

47. Greig and Springer, *The Kingdom and the Power*, 55-110.

48. Cardinal Leon Joseph Suenens, *A New Pentecost?* (New York, NY: The Seabury Press, 1975); Monsignor Vincent M. Walsh, *What Is Going On? Understand the Powerful Evangelism of Pentecostal Churches* (Wynnewood, PA: Key of David Publications, 1995); Monsignor Vincent M. Walsh, *Experiencing Revival in the Catholic Church: What God Is Doing in Our Midst—A Story of God's Initiative and Special Actions* (Wynnewood, PA: Key of David Publications, 1995); Ralph Martin, *The Catholic Church at the End of an Age: What is the Spirit Saying?* (San Francisco, CA: Ignatius Press, 1994); Bentivegna, "The Witness of St. Augustine"; Francis MacNutt, *The Healing Reawakening: Reclaiming Our Lost Inheritance* (Grand Rapids, MI: Chosen, 2005); Francis MacNutt, *Healing* (Notre Dame, IN: Ave Maria Press, 1974); Vladimir Lossky, *The Mystical Theology of the Eastern Church* (St. Vladimir Seminary Press, 1997); Gareth Leyshon, "Framing a Christian Response to New Age Practices: Core Issues and Pastoral Solutions," http://www.drgareth.info/NewAgeRP.pdf (accessed February 7, 2014); Gareth Leyshon, "A Catholic Critique of the Healing Art of Reiki," http://www.drgareth.info/Reiki_GL.pdf (accessed February 7, 2014); Kelsey, *Healing and Christianity*; Edward D. O'Connor, *The Pentecostal Movement in the Catholic Church* (Notre Dame, IN: Ave Maria Press, 1971).

49. Bentivegna, "The Witness of St. Augustine," 188-201, esp. 191.
50. Kelsey, *Healing and Christianity*, 187-88. Kelsey references *De Vera Religione, Cap* 25, nn 46, 47.
51. Augustine, *Retractationes*, 1, 13, 7; 1, 14, 5.
52. Bentivegna, "The Witness of St. Augustine," 188.
53. Ibid., 189, states: "One thing is certain: the outpouring of the pentecostal Spirit in the Church 'remains always an act of mercy and grace.' It is an act of mercy because it presupposes that those upon whom it flows 'have already received the forgiveness of their sins.' It is an act of grace because it has no relationship with the assessment of man's merits."
54. Ibid.
55. Ibid.
56. Ibid.,188-91.
57. Ibid., 191
58. Ibid., 192, citing Joannis Evangelium 32,7; cf. Sermo 267, 2-3.
59. Ibid., citing Sermo 269:1-2.
60. Ibid., citing Psalmum 67:16; cf. Confessiones 13, 14.
61. Ibid., 193-200.
62. Ibid.,193, citing De Genesi ad Litteram 12, 21, 44.
63. Ibid., citing Epistola 159, 5.
64. Ibid., 194, citing De Utilitate Credendi 16, 34.
65. Ibid., citing De Civitate Dei 22, 8, 1.
66. Ibid.
67. Ibid., citing Sermo 319,8,7; cf. Sermo 320. Augustine reflects the New Testament perspective on glory being brought to God through the working of healings and miracles.
68. Robert H. Culpepper, *Evaluating the Charismatic Movement: A Theological and Biblical Appraisal* (Valley Forge, PA: Judson Press, 1977), 83-85. His biblical reasons for rejecting cessationism are misunderstanding the perfect that is to come and limiting the purpose of the miraculous with authentication of the apostles when they were also an expression of the compassion of God. They were also a means of edifying the members of the body of Christ.

69. Roger Stronstad, *The Charismatic Theology of St. Luke* (Peabody, MA: Hendrickson Publishers, 1984).

70. Roger Stronstad, "Pentecostal Experience and Hermeneutics," *Enrichment Journal*, Assemblies of God USA, http://enrichmentjournal. ag.org/201004/201004_000_Pent_Herm.cfm (accessed February 7, 2014);

71. Bentivegna, "The Witness of St. Augustine," 189.

72. Lawrence Wood, *The Meaning of Pentecost in Early Methodism: Rediscovering John Fletcher as Wesley's Vindicator and Designated Successor* (Lanham, MD: Scarecrow Press Inc, 2002), 163-99.

73. Note the *"when you come together"* in 1 Corinthians 11:18, 20, 33, and 14:26.

74. Craig Keener, *A Commentary on the Gospel of Matthew* (Grand Rapids, MI: Eerdmans, 1999), 420.

75. Ibid., 421.

76. Note: John preferred to use the word *signs* for miracles and healings.

77. Accordance Bible Study Software, New American Standard Greek, Version 9.6, May 2012, Oak Tree Software, Inc.

78. Ibid.

79. Ruthven, *What's Wrong with Protestant Theology?*, 211n4. Ruthven questions Matthew the apostle, as the true author of the gospel that bears his name, because nowhere in the text is his name mentioned. It is based upon a fairly late tradition. Canonical, yes; written by Matthew, probably not. If you do include Matthew as written by Matthew, the percentage is just over 50 percent.

80. Ruthven, *On the Cessation of the Charismata*, 195; Greig and Springer, *The Kingdom and the Power,* 399-404.

81. Mark 16:20, "Then the disciples went out and preached everywhere, and the Lord worked with them and confirmed His word by the signs that accompanied it." What the signs confirm here is the word. The it is the word. The word is not a doctrine or a doctrinal system here; it is the gospel.

82. Ruthven, *What's Wrong with Protestant Theology?*, 203-240.

83. Guy Chevreau, *Catch the Fire: The Toronto Blessing* (London, UK: Marshall Pickering, 1994), 75-88.

84. Michael Brown, *Israel's Divine Healer* (Grand Rapids, MI: Zondervan, 1995), 29, 165.

85. Gustaf Aulén, *Christus Victor* (New York, NY: Macmillan, 1958).

86. Ruthven, *What's Wrong with Protestant Theology?*, 280-87.

87. Ibid., 284.

88. Ibid., 275-87.

89. Ibid., 289-98.

90. Clark, *Power, Holiness, and Evangelism.* This book is dedicated to the dual truth of the Spirit being poured out on Christians to not only give them power over their sinful flesh, but also power to evangelize, especially through the anointing and gifting of the Holy Spirit.

91. The official statement regarding the inspiration of the Bible for the Assemblies of God states under the heading "The Scriptures Inspired," "The Scriptures, both the Old and New Testaments, are verbally inspired of God and are the revelation of God to man, the infallible, authoritative rule of faith and conduct," http://ag.org/top/Beliefs/ Statement_of_fundamental_truths/sft_full.cfm#1 (accessed January 22, 2014).

The Church of God's official statement is, "The Church of God believes the whole Bible to be completely and equally inspired and that it is the written Word of God. The Church of God has adopted the following Declaration of Faith as its standard and official expression of its doctrine." It goes on, "We Believe: In the verbal inspiration of the Bible," http://www.churchofgod.org/index.php/pages/declairation-of-faith (accessed January 22, 2014).

The International Pentecostal Holiness Church states in its fifth statement of belief: "We believe in the verbal and plenary inspiration of the Holy Scriptures, known as the Bible, composed of sixty-six books and divided into two departments, Old and New Testaments. We believe the Bible is the Word of God, the full and complete revelation of the plan and history of redemption," http://www.iphc.org/beliefs (accessed January 22, 2014).

The Church of God in Christ, the largest African American Pentecostal denomination in America states, "We believe the Bible to be the inspired and only infallible written Word of God," http://www.cogic.org/ our-foundation/our-statement-of-faith/ (Accessed January 22, 2014).

92. Ruthven, *What's Wrong with Protestant Theology?*, 10n1; Ruthven, *On the Cessation of the Charismata*, 221-56.

93. The early church refuted the Montanists declaration that the prophet and prophetesses Montanus, Maximilla, and Priscilla, were the last prophets and that there would be no more prophecy after them. (This retraction was based upon 1 Corinthians 13:8, now used by cessationists to contradict the way the early church used it. They rejected this claim of Montanism because the text taught the gifts were to continue until the return of Jesus.) John Chapman, *The Catholic Encyclopedia*, vol. 10 (New York, NY: Robert Appleton, 1911), s.v. "Montanists," http://www.newadvent.org/cathen/10521a.htm (accessed June 29, 2013); See also Randy Clark, "The Relation of Faith to Healing and Miracles," in A Study of the Effects of Christian Prayer on Pain or Mobility Restrictions from Surgeries Involving Implanted Materials (D. Min. thesis, United Theological Seminary, 2013).

94. Ruthven, *On the Cessation of the Charismata*, 14.

95. Candy Gunther Brown, *Testing Prayer: Science and Healing* (Cambridge, MA: Harvard University Press, 2012), 60-61, 155-57, 161, 254-55.

96. Clark, "The Relation of Faith to Healing and Miracles," in *A Study of the Effects of Christian Prayer*, 49-68.

97. Exodus 14:4 says glory is connected to the miracle of deliverance from Egypt; Exodus 14:17 states that glory is revealed by defeating the Egyptian chariots and horsemen; Exodus 16:8 says that glory is due to the miracle of provision of food; Numbers 14:21-22 describes glory and signs; 1 Chronicles 16:24 shows how glory is connected to His marvelous works; Psalm 96:3 shows how His glory is connected to His marvelous works; Psalm 104:31 shows how glory is connected to His works; Isaiah 58:6-12 shows how ministry to the poor and oppressed causes healing to quickly appear, righteousness to go before us, and the glory of the Lord to become our rear guard; John 2:11 shows how glory was revealed by turning water into wine; in John 11:4, glory is connected to Lazarus's resurrection; John 11:40 shows that glory is connected to the resurrection of Lazarus, which was connected to the people's faith; John 12:37-41 shows how glory was connected to miraculous signs; John 14:13-14 shows believers bringing glory to the Father through doing what Jesus had done (miraculous deeds—in context, this passage is not limited to the apostles but to all believers); John 15:8 reveals that the Father's glory occurs through the disciples

bearing fruit (in context, the fruit is the fruit of doing—healing and miracles); John 16:14 shows how the Father brings glory to Jesus through His followers by revelatory gifts that create the faith for the working of miracles and healings; in John 17:4-5, Jesus brought glory to the Father by completing the work given to Him, inclusive of supernatural signs and wonders, healing and miracles; John 17:10 shows how glory came to Jesus through the disciples; John 17:22 reveals how Jesus gave the disciples the glory the Father had given Him (in context, the glory to work healings and miracles); in Romans 6:4, Jesus was raised through the glory of God; 1 Corinthians 15:43 shows that bodies are raised in general resurrection by the glory of God; Colossians 1:27 shows that Christ in us is the hope of glory—the hope of the power of God manifested through our lives by the gifts and anointing of the Spirit (both Paul and John used glory as a synonym for power); 1 Thessalonians 2:12 God calls us (present tense) into His Kingdom and glory; 1 Peter 4:13-14 shows that the Spirit of glory and of God rests upon the persecuted; in 2 Peter 1:16-18, transfiguration and the glory are connected—the implication is that the experience of glory prepares us not only for miracles, but for times of persecution or martyrdom. Through these references to glory, it is apparent there is a close connection between glory and healing, miracles, signs and wonders, and suffering persecution.

98. Gregory Boyd, "Historical Criticism of the Bible: Methodology or Ideology: Reflections of a Bultmannian turned Evangelical," *Christian Scholars Review* 22, no. 1 (1992), 106-109; Ken Blue, *Authority to Heal* (Downers Grove, IL: InterVarsity Press, 1987); Brown, *Israel's Divine Healer*; Johnson and Clark, *The Essential Guide to Healing*; Clark, *Power, Holiness, and Evangelism,* 51-74; Clark, *There Is More!*; Harvey Cox, *Fire From Heaven: The Rise of Pentecostal Spirituality and the Reshaping of Religion in the 21st Century* (Cambridge, MA: Da Capo Press, 1995); Mary Crawford, *The Shantung Revival: The Greatest Revival in Baptist Church History* (Mechanicsburg, PA: Global Awakening, 2005); Ern Crocker, *Ninety Minutes Past Midnight: A Medical Emergency Brings a Young Doctor Face to Face With His Not So Silent Partner* (Crownhill, Milton Keynes, UK: Authentic Media Limited, 2011); William DeArteaga, *Quenching the Spirit: Examining Centuries of Opposition to the Moving of the Holy Spirit* (Lake Mary, FL: Creation House, 1992); Jack Deere, *Surprised by the Power of the Spirit: Discovering How God Speaks and Heals Today* (Grand Rapids,

MI: Zondervan Publishing House, 1996); Deere, *Surprised by the Voice of God*; Doles, *Miracles and Manifestations*; Lewis A. Drummond, *The Awakening that Must Come* (Nashville, TN: Broadman Press, 1978); John Havlik and Lewis Drummond, *How Spiritual Awakenings Happen* (Nashville, TN: The Sunday School Board of the Southern Baptist Convention, 1981); Bob Ekblad, "Holistic Transformational Missions at the Margins," in *Supernatural Missions: The Impact of the Supernatural on World Missions*, ed. Randy Clark, (Mechanicsburg, PA: Global Awakening, 2012), 265-82; Howard M. Ervin, *Conversion-Initiation and the Baptism in the Holy Spirit: A Critique of James D. G. Dunn, Baptism in the Holy Spirit* (Peabody, MA: Hendrickson Publishers, Inc., 1984); Gordon Fee, *Gospel and Spirit: Issues in New Testament Hermeneutics* (Peabody, MA: Hendrickson Publishers, Inc, 1991); Gordon Fee, *God's Empowering Presence: The Holy Spirit in the Letters of Paul* (Peabody, MA: Hendrickson Publishers, 2009); Gordon Fee, *Paul, the Spirit, and the People of God* (Peabody, MA: Hendrickson Publishers, 1996); A. J. Gordon, *The Ministry of Healing: Or The Miracle of Cure for All Ages*, Third Edition Revised (New York, NY: Fleming B. Revell, 1882); Michael Green, *Evangelism in the Early Church* (Grand Rapids, MI: Eerdmans, 2003); Greig and Springer, *The Kingdom and the Power*; Hyatt, *2000 Years of Charismatic Christianity*; Philip Jenkins, *The Next Christendom: the Coming of Global Christianity* (New York, NY: Oxford University Press, 2002); Phillip E. Johnson, "The Unraveling of Scientific Materialism," *The Access Research Network—First Things Journal*, 1977, http://www.arn.org/ftissues/ft9711/articles/johnson.html (accessed July 16, 2013); Donald R. Kantel, *Downstream from Toronto: The "Toronto Blessing" Revival & Iris Ministries in Mozambique*, D. Min. dissertation (Virginia Beach, VA: Regent Divinity School, 2007): Keener, *Miracles*, 171-208; King, *Only Believe*; Paul King, "Supernatural Physical Manifestations in the Evangelical and Holiness Revival Movements," *The Pneuma Foundation: Resources for Spirit-Empowered Ministry*, Presented at the 32nd Society of Pentecostal Studies/Wesleyan Theological Society Joint Conference, March 21, 2003, History Interest Group, 2003 www.pneumafoundation.org/resources/articles/manifestations.pdf (accessed May 14, 2012); Byron D. Klaus, "Assemblies of God Theological Seminary," *Pentecostalism and Mission: Presented to the American Society of Missiology*, June 2006, http://www.agts.edu/faculty/faculty_publications/klaus/costa_rica/Pentecostalism_and_Mission.pdf (accessed May 19, 2012); Henry I. Lederle, *Theology with Spirit:*

Notes

*The Future of the Pentecostal-Charismatic Movements in the 21st Century* (Tulsa, OK: Word and Spirit Press, 2010); Ramsay MacMullen, *Christianizing The Roman Empire A.D. 100–400* (New Haven, CT: Yale University Press, 1984); MacNutt, *Healing*; MacNutt, *The Healing Reawakening*; Ralph Martin, *The Catholic Church at the End of an Age: What Is the Spirit Saying?* (San Francisco, CA: Ignatius Press, 1994); George Montague and Killian McDonnell, *Christian Initiation and Baptism in the Holy Spirit*; Gary B. McGee, "Miracles and Missions Revisited," *International Bulletin of Missionary Research*, October 2001, 146-56, esp. 154-55; McIntyre, *E. W. Kenyon*; Bentivegna, "The Witness of St. Augustine;"; Donald Miller, "The New Face of Global Christianity: The Emergence of 'Progressive Pentecostalism,'" *The Pew Forum on Religion and Public Life* (Washington, D. C.: The Pew Research Center, 2011); J. P. Moreland, *Kingdom Triangle: Recover the Christian Mind Renovate the Soul Restore the Spirit's Power* (Grand Rapids, MI: Zondervan, 2007); Mark A. Noll, *The New Shape of World Christianity* (Downers Grove, IL: IVP Academic, 2009); Mark Pearson, *Christian Healing: A Comprehensive and Practical Guide* (Lake Mary, FL: Charisma House, 2004); Lynette F. Hoelter and Margaret M. Poloma, "The Toronto Blessing: A Holistic Model of Healing," *Journal for the Scientific Study of Religion* 37 no. 2 (1998): 257-75; Pontifical Council For Culture Pontifical Council for Interreligious Dialogue, *Jesus Christ The Bearer Of The Water Of Life: A Christian Reflection on the "New Age,"* http://www.vatican.va/roman_curia/pontifical_councils/interelg/documents/rc_pc_interelg_doc_20030203_new-age_en.html (accessed March 5, 2012); Amanda Porterfield, *Healing in the History of Christianity* (New York, NY: Oxford University Press, 2005); Winkie Pratney, *Revival—Its Principles and Personalities*; Charles Price, *The Real Faith: Original Pentecostal Classics Edition with Introduction by Tim Enloe* (Wichita, KS: EM Publications, 2008); David Pytches, *Prophecy in the Local Church* (London, UK: Hodder and Stougton, 1993); Michael Donald Richardson, *Lessons from the Revival in Argentina*, D. Min. dissertation (Pasadena, CA: Fuller Theological Seminary, 1998); Ruthven, *On the Cessation of the Charismata*; Ruthven, *What's Wrong with Protestant Theology?*; Noberto Sarraco, "The Holy Spirit and the Church's Mission of Healing," *International Review of Mission* (The American Theological Library Association) 93, 370-371 (July-Oct 2004), 413-20; Gary Shogren, "Christian Prophecy and Canon in the Second Century: A Response to B. B. Warfield," *Journal of the Evangelical Theological Society* (Evangelical Theological Society) 40,

215

no. 4 (December 1977), 609-26; Gary Shogren, "First Corinthians: An exegetical-pastoral commentary," Gary Shogren, n.d., http://openoureyeslord.files.wordpress.com/2012/05/shogren_1_corinthians.pdf (accessed April 29, 2013); Gary Shogren, "How Did They Suppose 'The Perfect Would Come? 1 Corinthians 13.8-12 In Patristic Exegesis?" *Journal of Pentecostal Theology* (BRILL) 15 (1999), 99-121; Mark Stibbe, *Times of Refreshing: A Practical Theology of Revival for Today* (London, UK: Marshall Pickering, 1995); Stronstad, "Pentecostal Experience and Hermeneutics Enrichment Journal"; Stronstad, *The Charismatic Theology of St. Luke*; (Grand Rapids, MI: Baker Academic, 1990); Thomas F. Tracy, ed., *God Who Acts: Philosophical and Theological Explorations* (University Park, PA: Pennsylvania State University Press, 1994); Alexander Venter, *Doing Healing: How to Minister God's Kingdom in the Power of the Spirit* (Cape Town, South Africa: Vineyard International Publishing, 2009); Rich Nathan and Gary Wilson, *Empowered Evangelicals: Bringing Together the Best of the Evangelical and Charismatic Worlds* (Ann Arbor, Michigan: Vine Books, 1995); John Wimber, *Power Healing* (San Francisco, CA: Harper and Row Publishers, 1987); Laurence W. Wood, *The Meaning of Pentecost in Early Methodism*; (Lanham, MD: Scarecrow Press, 2002); Henry Worsley, *The Life of Martin Luther in Two Volumes* (1856); Friedrich Zuendel, *The Awakening: One Man's Battle With Darkness* (Farmington, PA: The Plough Publishing Company, 1999).

99. Ruthven, *What's Wrong with Protestant Theology?*, 3-4.

100. Ibid.

101. See Ezra 3:11, Job 33:26, Psalm 27:6, 33:3, 42:4, 47:1, 66:1, 71:23, 81:1, 95:1, 98:4, 100:1, Isaiah 48:20, Zechariah 9:9, Matthew 21:9, 21:15, John 12:13, Revelation 19:1.

102. See Exodus 15:20, 1 Samuel 18:6, 2 Samuel 6:14, 16, Psalm 30:11, 149:3, 150:4, Ecclesiastes 3:4, Jeremiah 31:4, Luke 15:25.

103. See Genesis 24:52, 1 Chronicles 29:20, 2 Chronicles 20:18, Psalm 95:6.

104. Psalm 28:2, 63:4, 119:48, 134:2, 141:2.

105. John 4:23-24: "Yet a time is coming and has now come when the true worshipers will worship the Father in spirit and truth, for they are the kind of worshipers the Father seeks. God is spirit, and His worshipers must worship in spirit and in truth."

106. For a biblical, historical, and contemporary analysis of the concept of impartation, see my book *There Is More!* The two-fold purpose of this

book was to defend the biblical doctrine of laying on of hands (i.e., impartation), and the outpouring of the Spirit at Toronto that became known as the Toronto Blessing. This apologetic was written to show how cessationism developed and what God did to bring the church back from its anemic state to living once again in the power of the Spirit. The fruit of the outpouring was examined by studying the lives of people who were transformed by a divine encounter. The fruit of their ministries was studied in order to discern properly whether this was a good tree or a bad tree.

107. See John 20:22 and Acts 1:5,8; 2:4,38, 4:31, 8:15-19, 9:17.

108. Original NIV emphasis.

109. Wood, *The Meaning of Pentecost in Early Methodism*, 357-79, esp. 361.

110. These are the three most common periods used for the termination of the "sign" gifts. There is disagreement among cessationists about when the gifts ended. Related to this passage is the largely overlooked general statement: *"God works in all of them in all men* [Greek: *charismata*]*"* (1 Cor. 12:6).

111. Jon Ruthven, e-mail message to author, April 3, 2013.

112. "I always thank God for you because of His grace given you in Christ Jesus. For in Him you have been enriched in every way—in all your speaking and in all your knowledge—because our testimony about Christ was confirmed in you. Therefore you do not lack any spiritual gift as you eagerly wait for our Lord Jesus Christ to be revealed. He will continue to confirm you to the end, so that you will be blameless on the day of our Lord Jesus Christ" (1 Cor. 1:4-8). These verses stress the continuation of all the gifts until Jesus Christ is revealed. Paul said the Christians were not to lack "any" gift as they wait for the revelation of Jesus Christ. This is scriptural evidence for believing in the continuation of the gifts until Jesus comes again. Crucially important is the promise that "He will continue to confirm" (presumably in the same charismatic way) "to the end." The Greek word for "confirm" is bebaioō, which is clearly used in the New Testament as miraculous or charismatic revelation establishing faith (see Mark 16:20; Rom. 15:8; 1 Cor. 1:6, 8; 2 Cor. 1:22-23; Heb. 2:3-4). Karl Rengstorf, *Theological Dictionary of the New Testament*, ed. Gerhard Kittel and Gerhard Friedrich, trans. Geoffrey W. Bromiley (Grand Rapids, MI: Eerdmans, 1977), s.v., "bebaioō," 1:600-603. Thiselton sees the introductory passage of 1 Corinthians 4–8 as a key to understanding 1 Cor. 13:8-10.

Anthony C. Thiselton, *First Corinthians: A Shorter Exegetical and Pastoral Commentary* (Grand Rapids, MI: Eerdmans, 2006), location 497-500, Kindle ebook.

"Does God give you His Spirit and work miracles among you because you observe the law, or because you believe what you heard?" (Gal. 3:5). This is a poor translation, making the focus of miracles on the believers' believing the preached word. A translation that better captures the true dynamic of faith and miracles in the New Testament would be the Revised Standard Version: "Does He who supplies the Spirit to you and works miracles among you do so by works of the law, or by hearing with faith?" In the King James Version, it is translated as, "He therefore that ministereth to you the Spirit, and worketh miracles among you, doeth He it by the works of the law, or by the hearing of faith?" Young's Literal Translation of the New Testament also translates "or by the hearing of faith?"

This passage indicates that the churches in Galatia that Paul, who was their spiritual father, founded had experienced and were experiencing miracles in their churches. The verb tense is present, not past, and would imply that the miraculous nature of the life of the church continued even when their apostle was not present among them. It is significant that the miracles are wrought by the hearing of faith. This is not the same as believing what one has heard, indicating believing in the preached gospel. This is what saved them, but it is not what releases the miracles. It is the preaching to others accompanied by the hearing of faith of the already saved new believers that causes the miracles and healing. This hearing of faith encompasses hearing the directives from the Holy Spirit—whether it is receiving words of knowledge that create the faith to declare the will of the Lord in the particular situation or the "hearing of faith" that refers to experiencing the gift of faith, either way it is not the gospel the disciples are hearing. Rather, it is the gospel they are declaring as they experience the hearing of faith—the operation of gifts of the Spirit—which, in turn, creates the faith for the operation of healing and miracles. The point is the hearing of faith that produces the miracles and healing. It is the rhema they are hearing, not the kerygma. They came into the Kingdom by believing what they heard, the gospel, the kerygma; but they now advance the Kingdom by the hearing of faith—freshly spoken directives from the Lord through the Spirit, enabling signs and wonders to accompany the preaching of the gospel, confirming it with signs and wonders: "Then the disciples went out and preached everywhere, and the Lord worked with them and confirmed His word by the signs that accompanied it" (Mark 16:20).

113. Shogren, "How Did They Suppose 'The Perfect' Would Come?;" Shogren, "First Corinthians;" Anthony C Thiselton, *The Holy Spirit: In Biblical Teaching, Through the Centuries, and Today* (Grand Rapids, MI: Eerdmans, 2013); Thiselton, *First Corinthians.* In Thiselton's larger commentary, *First Epistle,* he discusses in greater depth the issue of cessationist views of tongues, 1061-64; Gordon D. Fee, *The First Epistle to the Corinthians: The New International Commentary on the New Testament* (Grand Rapids, MI: Eerdmans, 1987); I. Howard Marshall, *New Testament Theology: Many Witnesses, One Gospel* (Downers Grove, IL: InterVarsity Press, 2004), 3, Kindle ebook.

114. Randy Clark, ed., "Healing and the Glory of God," in *Empowered: A School of Healing and Impartation Workbook* (Mechanicsburg, PA: Global Awakening, 2012), 191-201. A study of the word *glory* in the Hebrew and the Greek shows that the main way God glorifies His name is through signs and wonders, miracles and healings. This correlation of glory and miracles was higher than any other category. Clark, *Empowered,* 192-94. The second highest dealt with the pillar of fire by night and the cloud by day of the Exodus wanderings. Nothing else even came close.

115. "But to each one of us grace has been given as Christ apportioned it. This is why it says: 'When He ascended on high, He led captives in His train and gave gifts to men.' (What does 'He ascended' mean except that He also descended to the lower, earthly regions? He who descended is the very One who ascended higher than all the heavens, in order to fill the whole universe.) It was He who gave some to be apostles, some to be prophets, some to be evangelists, and some to be pastors and teachers, to prepare God's people for works of service, so that the body of Christ may be built up until we all reach unity in the faith and in the knowledge of the Son of God and become mature, attaining to the whole measure of the fullness of Christ" (Eph. 4:7-13).

This passage teaches that the office gifts of apostles, prophets, evangelists, pastors, and teachers were to continue, "until we all reach unity in the faith and in the knowledge of the Son of God and become mature, attaining to the whole measure of the fullness of Christ." Now that we have determined the duration of these office gifts, let us determine their purpose. Their purpose was to "prepare God's people for works of service, so that the body of Christ may be built up." This is still a need in the church today.

"And do not grieve the Holy Spirit of God, with whom you were sealed for the day of redemption" (Eph. 4:30). The Holy Spirit's sealing was unto the day of redemption. I believe we can grieve Him by not listening to Him, ignoring Him, and not exercising His "gracelets"—His grace packages to us.

116. Two passages make this clear: "But as surely as God is faithful, our message to you is not 'Yes' and 'No.' For the Son of God, Jesus Christ, who was preached among you by me and Silas and Timothy, was not 'Yes' and 'No,' but in Him it has always been 'Yes.' For no matter how many promises God has made, they are 'Yes' in Christ. And so through Him the 'Amen' is spoken by us to the glory of God" (2 Cor. 1:18-20). And, "It is written: 'I believed; therefore I have spoken.' With that same spirit of faith we also believe and therefore speak" (2 Cor. 4:13).

117. "The end of all things is near. Therefore be clear minded and self-controlled so that you can pray. Above all, love each other deeply, because love covers over a multitude of sins. Offer hospitality to one another without grumbling. Each one should use whatever gift he has received to serve others, faithfully administering God's grace in its various forms. If anyone speaks, he should do it as one speaking the very words of God. If anyone serves, he should do it with the strength God provides, so that in all things God may be praised through Jesus Christ. To Him be the glory and the power forever and ever. Amen" (1 Pet. 4:7-11).

118. "I am writing these things to you about those who are trying to lead you astray. As for you, the anointing you received from Him remains in you, and you do not need anyone to teach you. But as His anointing teaches you about all things and as that anointing is real, not counterfeit—just as it has taught you, remain in Him" (1 John 2:26-27).

119. Ruthven, *On the Cessation of the Charismata*, 102-107; Greig and Springer, *The Kingdom and the Power*, 399-403; William Kurz, "Chapter Four: Sharing Jesus' Power for Service," in *Following Jesus: A Disciple's Guide to Luke-Acts* (Ann Arbor, MI: Servant Books, 1984), 57-67. Kurz implies in the introduction on page 5 that these early commissions in Luke 9 and 10 were intended by Luke to apply beyond the early disciples mentioned there to Luke's readers generally.

See also Don Williams, *Signs, Wonders and the Kingdom of God* (Ann Arbor, MI: Servant Books, 1989), 125; Charles Kraft, *Christianity with Power* (Ann Arbor, MI: Servant Books, 1989), 136.

Colin Brown argues that because the specific commission was brief and limited to the Jews at that time, the commands to heal and exorcise demons can have no application to the later reader. Colin Brown, "The Other Half of the Gospel," *Christianity Today* 33 (April 1989), 27. This is clearly not the pattern in the book of Acts, in the summary statements of Paul's mission, or in the passages investigated by Ruthven in *On the Cessation of the Charismata*, 103n10.

120. Tom Jones, *"Divine Encounters: Analysis of Encounters that Shape Lives"* (D. Min. thesis, United Theological Seminary, 2013).

121. Ibid. See Appendix A for the positive results of Dr. Jones' study of the effects of encounters with God.

# ABOUT THE AUTHOR

Randy Clark is the President and Founder of Global Awakening. Established in 1994, Global Awakening is an apostolic ministry that aims to equip the body of Christ through ministry schools, training programs, conferences and international mission trips. Through his ministry, Randy has seen tens of thousands healed and brought to salvation.

In 1994, this unassuming pastor from St. Louis walked into a small storefront church near the Toronto airport. Originally scheduled for four days, his meetings turned into a worldwide revival known as the Toronto Blessing, which resulted in four million conversions and over 20,000 church plants worldwide.

Dr. Clark received his M.Div. from The Southern Baptist Theological Seminary and his D.Min. from United Theological Seminary where he completed a doctorate thesis both theologically and medically verifying healing. He also received a Th.D. from the Phoenix University of Theology. Randy has authored and co-authored numerous books, training manuals and workbooks, including There Is More! and The Essential Guide to Healing. Noted primarily for revivals associated with healing and impartation, Randy has ministered for more than 44 years in 50 nations. He lives in Mechanicsburg, PA with his wife, DeAnne. They have four grown children and four grandchildren.

# LEARN TO MINISTER AS JESUS DID.

*"Christian Healing Certification Program is sure to help people come into a greater understanding of this vital area of ministry. And even more important is that participants will have greater fruitfulness for the glory of God. I highly recommend this training program. It will change your life."*

**-BILL JOHNSON, BETHEL CHURCH, REDDING, CA**

Do you feel a stirring in your heart to take the next step in preparation for ministry? Do you want to see healing and deliverance operating in your own life? Join us for one of our online classes in the areas of Physical Healing, Deliverance or Inner Healing.

**No Prior training necessary**

**Courses are available to fit your schedule**

**Small and personal classes of 15-17 students per class**

**It's easy and can be done right from home**

**Economical and inexpensive**

**Join a community of online students from all over the world**

**Over one thousand people have completed coursework**

For more information or to register, visit our website at **www.healingcertification.com** or call **717.796.9866 X124**. Most materials avaiable at global Awakening Bookstore.

**CHCP** Christian Healing CERTIFICATION PROGRAM

Made in the USA
Columbia, SC
29 October 2022

70187816R00124